Opposing Viewpoints

David L. Bender

OPPOSING VIEWPOINTS SERIES

**THIRD
EDITION**

Greenhaven Press

577 SHOREVIEW PARK ROAD
ST. PAUL, MINNESOTA 55112

Third revised and extended edition

ISBN 0-89908-305-6 Paper Edition
ISBN 0-89908-330-7 Library Edition

CONGRESS SHALL MAKE NO LAW... ABRIDGING THE FREEDOM OF SPEECH, OR OF THE PRESS

first amendment to the U.S. Constitution

The basic foundation of our democracy is the first amendment guarantee of freedom of expression. The OPPOSING VIEWPOINTS SERIES is dedicated to the concept of this basic freedom and the idea that it is more important to practice it than to enshrine it.

TABLE OF CONTENTS

the Opposing viewpoints series

THE IMPORTANCE OF EXAMINING OPPOSING VIEWPOINTS

The purpose of this book, and the Opposing Viewpoints Series as a whole, is to confront you with alternative points of view on complex and sensitive issues.

Perhaps the best way to inform yourself is to analyze the positions of those who are regarded as experts and well studied on the issues. It is important to consider every variety of opinion in an attempt to determine the truth. Opinions from the mainstream of society should be examined. Also important are opinions that are considered radical, reactionary, minority or stigmatized by some other uncomplimentary label. An important lesson of history is the fact that many unpopular opinions eventually became the majority opinion of the day. The opinions of Socrates, Jesus and Galileo are good examples of this.

You will approach this book with opinions of your own on the issues debated within it. To have a good grasp of your own viewpoint you must understand the arguments of those with whom you disagree. It is said that those who do not completely understand their adversary's point of view do not fully understand their own.

Perhaps the most persuasive case for considering opposing viewpoints has been presented by John Stuart Mill in his work *On Liberty*. Consider the following statements of his when studying controversial issues.

THE OPINIONS OF OTHERS

If all mankind minus one were of one opinion, and only one person were of the contrary opinion, mankind would be no more justified in silencing that one person than he, if he had the power, would be justified in silencing mankind....

We can never be sure that the opinion we are endeavoring to stifle is a false opinion...

All silencing of discussion is an assumption of infallibility....

Ages are no more infallible than individuals; every age having held many opinions which subsequent ages have deemed not only false but absurd; and it is as certain that many opinions now general will be rejected by future ages....

The only way in which a human being can make some approach to knowing the whole of a subject, is by hearing what can be said about it by persons of every variety of opinion, and studying all modes in which it can be looked at by every character of mind. No wise man ever acquired his wisdom in any mode but this....

The beliefs which we have most warrant for have no safeguard to rest on but a standing invitation to the whole world to prove them unfounded....

To call any proposition certain, while there is any one who would deny its certainty if permitted, but who is not permitted, is to assume that we ourselves and those who agree with us are the judges of certainty, and judges without hearing the other side....

Men are not more zealous for truth than they are for error, and a sufficient application of legal or even social penalties will generally succeed in stopping the propagation of either....

However unwilling a person who has a strong opinion may admit the possibility that his opinion may be false, he ought to be moved by the consideration that, however true it may be, if it is not fully, frequently, and fearlessly discussed, it will be a dead dogma, not a living truth.

I would like to point out to younger readers that John Stuart Mill lived in an era that was not sensitive to terms many people today consider sexist. The words *man* and *mankind* were often used in his work as synonyms for *people* and *humankind*.

A pitfall to avoid in considering alternative points of view is that of regarding your own point of view as being merely common sense and the most rational stance, and the point of view of others as being only opinion and naturally wrong. It may be that the opinion of others is correct and that yours is in error.

Another pitfall to avoid is that of closing your mind to the opinions of those whose views differ from yours. The best way to approach a dialogue is to make your primary purpose that of understanding the mind and arguments of the other person and not that of enlightening him or her with your solutions. One learns more by listening than by speaking.

It is my hope that after reading this book you will have a deeper understanding of the issues debated and will appreciate the complexity of even seemingly simple issues when good and honest people disagree. This awareness is particularly important in a democratic society such as ours, where people enter into public debate to determine the common good. People with whom you disagree should not be regarded as enemies, but rather as friends who suggest a different path to a common goal.

I would also like to caution you about being unwilling to take a stand on an issue because of a lack of information. You should always be ready to form an opinion from the facts at hand. You should also remain flexible and be able to alter your opinion when new facts justify it.

ANALYZING SOURCES OF INFORMATION

The Opposing Viewpoints Series uses diverse sources; magazines, journals, books, newspapers, statements and position papers from a wide range of individuals and organizations. These sources help in the development of a mindset that is open to the consideration of a variety of opinions.

The format of the Opposing Viewpoints Series should help you answer the following questions.

1. *Are you aware that three of the most popular weekly news magazines, Time, Newsweek, and U.S. News and World Report are not totally objective accounts of the news?*

2. **Do you know there is no such thing as a completely objective author, book, newspaper or magazine?**

3. **Do you think that because a magazine or newspaper article is unsigned it is always a statement of facts rather than opinions?**

4. **How can you determine the point of view of newspapers and magazines?**

5. **When you read do you question an author's frame of reference (political persuasion, training, and life experience)?**

Many people finish their formal education unable to cope with these basic questions. They have little chance to understand the social forces and issues surrounding them. Some fall easy victims to demagogues preaching solutions to problems by scapegoating minorities with conspiratorial and paranoid explanations of complex social issues.

I do not want to imply that anything is wrong with authors and publications that have a political slant or bias. All authors have a frame of reference. Readers should understand this. You should also understand that almost all writers have a point of view. An important skill in reading is to be able to locate and identify a point of view. This series gives you practice in both.

DEVELOPING BASIC THINKING SKILLS

A number of basic skills for critical thinking are practiced in the discussion activities that appear throughout the books in the series. Some of the skills are:

Locating a Point of View The ability to determine which side of an issue an author supports.

Evaluating Sources of Information The ability to choose from among alternative sources the most reliable and accurate source in relation to a given subject.

Distinguishing Between Primary and Secondary Sources The ability to understand the important distinction between sources which are primary (original or eyewitness accounts) and those which are secondary (historically removed from, and based on, primary sources).

Separating Fact from Opinion The ability to make the basic distinction between factual statements (those which can be demonstrated or verified empirically) and statements of opinion (those which are beliefs or attitudes that cannot be proved).

Distinguishing Between Prejudice and Reason The ability to differentiate between statements of prejudice (unfavorable, preconceived judgments based on feelings instead of reason) and statements of reason (conclusions that can be clearly and logically explained or justified).

Identifying Stereotypes The ability to identify oversimplified, exaggerated descriptions (favorable or unfavorable) about people, often insulting statements about racial, religious or national groups, and based on misinformation or lack of information.

Recognizing Ethnocentrism The ability to recognize attitudes or opinions that express the view that one's own race, culture, or group is inherently superior, or those attitudes that judge another race, culture, or group in terms of one's own.

It is important to consider opposing viewpoints. It is equally important to be able to critically analyze those viewpoints. The discussion activities in this book will give you practice in mastering these thinking skills.

Using this book, and others in the series, will help you develop critical thinking skills. These skills should improve your ability to better understand what you read. You should be better able to separate fact from opinion, reason from rhetoric. You should become a better consumer of information in our media-centered culture.

A VALUES ORIENTATION

Throughout the Opposing Viewpoints Series you are presented conflicting values. A good example is *American Foreign Policy*. The first chapter debates whether foreign policy should be based on the same kind of moral principles that individuals use in guiding their personal actions, or instead be based primarily on doing what best advances national interests, regardless of moral implications.

Some people advocate that values be kept out of the classroom. This series takes a different position. I believe that a consideration of basic values and principles is necessary before specific issues can be meaningfully examined and debated. How can you decide issues like capital punishment, abortion, welfare assistance, natural resource management or any other controversial issue before you give some thought to a general life philosophy? The way you answer the question "What is the meaning of life?" will have a great bearing on how you answer the question "How should society deal with murderers?" Because of this consideration all books in the series feature viewpoints and discussion activities that challenge you to constantly re-examine and reformulate your basic values.

The series does not advocate a particular set of values. It is left to you to formulate the values orientation that you find most suitable. My concern, as editor of the series, is to see that a wide range of viewpoints is fairly presented.

David L. Bender
Opposing Viewpoints Series Editor

THE PROBLEM OF PRISONS

Prisons are a major social problem. Some believe that prisons should deal more harshly with criminals. They think crime would be deterred and society better protected by punishing criminals with stiffer sentences. Others feel that punishment is never justified, because it creates even more anger and frustration in personalities that are already disorganized. They claim that society is more endangered than protected by inmates who are alienated by punitive prison systems and then released after serving their sentences.

What are prison conditions like in America today? Do prisons protect society and rehabilitate prisoners? Should punishment be part of a prison sentence? What should be the purpose of prisons? These and other questions are explored in this book. The prison official, the inmate, the psychiatrist, the journalist, and others speak in this volume. Consider their ideas carefully and make your own decisions about America's prisons.

Chapter **1**

AMERICA'S PRISONS

What are Prisons Like?

Are prisons doing their job?
How much do you know about the
way prisons really work?
Try giving yourself this short quiz!

A PRISON POLL

Phil Harnden

Instructions

Assume that you are a prisoner in an American prison. Try to answer the following ten questions to the best of your ability. The answers appear on page 142.

1. On any given day, about _____ Americans like me are held in correctional institutions.
   a. 48,000
   b. 121,000
   c. 318,000
   d. 568,000

2. In 1976, the average annual cost of caring for and keeping a prisoner like me was
   a. $1,200.
   b. $6,500.
   c. $11,000.
   d. $20,000.

3. Constructing and financing a hundred-bed minimum security facility for prisoners like me costs
   a. $25,000 per bed.
   b. $50,000 per bed.
   c. $75,000 per bed.
   d. $100,000 per bed.

Phil Harnden,"I Was A Prisoner And...," *The Other Side*, February 1979. Reprinted with permission from *The Other Side*, Box 12236, Philadelphia, PA 19144. The factual data in the poll was obtained from *In These Times*, National Council on Crime and Delinquency and National Moratorium on Prison Construction.

4. If I had been convicted in another industrialized nation instead of the U.S., my sentence would probably have been
a. longer.
b. shorter.
c. about the same.

5. A 1976 study by the Congressional Budget Office revealed that nearly all of the variation in federal prison intake could be explained by changes in
a. gun control laws.
b. the rate of unemployment.
c. the political party controlling Congress.
d. none of the above.

6. Nearly one-third of my fellow inmates were _____ before their latest arrest.
a. unemployed
b. drunk
c. politicians
d. drunk politicians

7. It would seem that the best way to keep people like me out of prison is to give them
a. guns.
b. better lawyers.
c. jobs.
d. deterrents, like the certainty of stiff sentences.

8. A study done in California prisons found that convicts who served a less-than-average-length sentence fared _____ on the outside than did matched convicts who served longer-than-average-length sentences.
a. better
b. worse
c. no differently

9. A 1974 study for the Ohio Youth Commission found that youths with the longest stay in prison
a. came from fatherless homes.
b. were the most interested in changing their life styles.
c. had the highest rate of return.
d. learned their lesson and rarely broke the law again.

10. Of the one hundred "rehabilitated" state prisoners paroled with me, _____ will probably return to prison someday.
a. less than ten
b. between fifteen and twenty
c. at least thirty-five
d. fifty-eight

"We may have committed a crime, but are we not still human beings with the right to be treated as such?"

Prison Is Dehumanizing

Clarence Billingsley

Clarence Billingsley wrote this article while in his fifteenth year of a life term for murder at Rahway State Prison in New Jersey. He has since been released from prison.

Consider the following questions while reading:
1. **Why does the author feel convicts lose their individuality in prison?**
2. **Why do prisoners learn to hate, in the author's opinion?**

Clarence Billingsley, "Prison Is Where...," *Corrections Magazine*, September 1979. Copyright 1979 by Criminal Justice Publications. Reprinted with permission from *Corrections Magazine*.

PRISON IS WHERE...

Prison is where you're issued one roll of toilet tissue per month per man and you run out on the 29th, and come down with a case of diarrhea on the 30th, and then are told that you'll have to wait until the 1st for the monthly supplies. It is eating badly prepared food until the senses of smell and taste no longer matter.

Prison is where you are broken down and rebuilt. You are told what to do, when to do it, how to do it, and the time in which you are to do it. It is a place where it becomes very unhealthy to even think. To think is to realize what is being done to you, to go insane if you do not have the fortitude to withstand the process of harassment and dehumanization. Some get high regularly on drugs, "hooch," or whatever they can get to escape the reality of it all. Some get involved with homos and play house in order to maintain identities of masculinity. Most choose not to think, and in doing so become what is asked of them—mechanical men, moving from day to day without thought, purpose, or a will of their own.

YOU LOSE INDIVIDUALITY

Prison is where you're told to "act like a man" and are treated like a child. And when you remind those in authority that you are not a child and you do not appreciate being treated as such, you're "insubordinate." If you maintain your individuality as a man you're labeled a "troublemaker." On the other hand, if you give up your individuality, scratch your head, skin and grin, and become docile, you are well behaved and a model prisoner.

Prison is where you're judged and labeled, not because of what you have done or what you are, but because of who your friends are. If you are not a junkie, and your friends are junkies, you are a junkie—guilt by association. Prison is where another prisoner can dislike you and because of his dislike, jealousy, envy and fear of you, drops a note to a guard that states you have contraband in your cell. And without consideration of the source or validity of the statement, the authorities will come and tear your cell apart looking for something, something that was never there in the first place. And for them to apologize for disrupting your cell and peace of mind is unthinkable, for you are a prisoner.

Prison is where you're allowed to receive contact visits from your loved ones. You're permitted to kiss your wife, or girlfriend, to hold them in your arms and whisper in their ears. But don't let your hand touch her thigh or linger too long on her breast, lest you violate prison rule 051, "Engaging in Sexual Acts With Others."

Prison is where you're allowed to earn "minimum" status and in doing so, you're trusted to work around the public. But you're forbidden to speak to them, even if they speak to you. If you fail to comply with this rule, you'll be charged with violating rule .702, "Unauthorized Contact With The Public," for which you could lose your minimum status. When you go to the zoo, there's a sign: "Don't feed the animals."

"MY NUMBER IS TWENTY-ZERO-TWENTY, BUT YOU CAN CALL ME TWENTY FOR SHORT."

YOU LEARN TO HATE

Prison is where you're told to have respect for those in authority. But instead of respect, you learn to hate, because you're treated less than human, and held in contempt by those in authority, simply because you are a prisoner. You also learn to control and suppress that hate, for prison is no place for hatred. In being a prisoner, you don't have the right to display or express your feelings.

We exist from one year to the next. For what? Parole! And when that day finally arrives, parole is denied. "You have not done enough time for the crime that you commited." "Society is not ready to accept you back into its fold. Come and see us again in a year." Over and over, until all of our hopes and dreams have been shattered. Like zombies we move from day to day, month to month, year to year. Some looking for reasons why they are in prison, others not caring.

YOU WAIT

We wait and watch, while the weaker ones go insane because the pain is unbearable. We wait to hear from families and loved ones that no longer care.

I am not saying that there should be crime without punishment, or that the doors of prisons should be thrown open and everyone let out. What I am saying is that we are not born thieves and murderers; we are indoctrinated and influenced by society. Some of us are thieves and murderers only because of extenuating circumstances. Some of us are made compulsive by some disorder or another that causes us to do the things we have done. And worst of all, there are those of us who commit crimes for the pure enjoyment of it, and the thrill derived from doing so. And society puts us in prison without any method or attempt at seeking the causes, diagnosing the illness, and dealing with the solution that would help us as well as society in the process.

We may have committed a crime, but are we not still human beings with the right to be treated as such? In losing our freedom, being deprived the right to exercise our manhood, and the suppression of our pride and dignity, do we not at least have the right to also live as human beings?

YOU RETURN TO SOCIETY

We are your problem, and storing us in prison isn't an answer or a solution to solving that problem, only a temporary retreat. For without the proper treatment, and unless an individual has the fortitude and incentive to better himself and his condition while in prison, he will return to society—a little wiser, a lot older, and bitter as hell—to revive and enlarge upon a problem that you diagnosed and prescribed, but neglected to treat. If by some miracle a person manages to survive the depressing, degrading, and dehumanizing conditions of prison life, and returns to society with the intention of living and leading a normal life, he will retain some bitterness from his prison experience. And no doubt obtain more bitterness from society, for society will alienate and reject him because he has been in prison, instead of offering an understanding and helping hand.

Prison is where you're issued one roll of toilet paper per month per man. And you run out on the 29th, and come down with a case of diarrhea on the 30th, and you are told that you'll have to wait...

THE ANGOLITE

For a firsthand account of what prison is like you may want to subscribe to The Angolite, *published by the inmates of Louisiana State Penitentiary. In describing the magazine in its April 2, 1980 issue,* Time *referred to* The Angolite *as "the most probing and literate inmate publication in the U.S.". An annual subscription of 6 issues is $5. Send to:*
The Angolite
c/o Cashier's Office
Louisiana State Prison
Angola, LA 70712

"Prisons and jails are slowly changing, and I believe for the better. Inmates have more rights than ever before and while progress is admittedly slow, institutions are being made more humane and safe."

PRISONS ARE IMPROVING

Norman Carlson

Norman Carlson is the Director of the *Federal Bureau of Prisons*. He made the following statement on Law Day, May 1, 1978 in Clearwater, Florida.

Consider the following questions while you read:
1. **Why does the author claim prisoner's rights have improved since the 1960's?**
2. **What does the author refer to when using the term "hands-off doctrine"?**
3. **Why is funding for prisons put at the bottom of the list according to the author?**

PRISONER'S RIGHTS

I believe that the most effective agent of change in our society is the law.

This judgment is based not only on the changes in law made by the Congress and the various State legislatures — important as these have been — but primarily on the development of law stemming from decisions made by the courts of this nation. Laws to protect and enlarge the rights of individuals, of minorities, of women, of prisoners and of other submerged groups in our population have been grounded in a new and fairer vision of Constitutional rights proclaimed in recent times by the courts.

Since the legal profession first began observing Law Day 17 years ago, a tremendous change has taken place with respect to the courts and corrections, as part of a wider movement to protect the rights of all citizens. Up to the early 1960's, prisoners had few rights. Their access to courts and attorneys was limited. Their mail could be withheld and censored, and nobody was particularly upset if their religious rights and other liberties were curtailed. The courts maintained a "hands-off" posture towards inmate rights and inmate suits. The courts adopted this doctrine for what seemed like three very good reasons. The first was the separation of powers, which was interpreted as meaning that the executive branch alone was responsible for prisons, except for funding. Secondly, the courts felt they lacked the expertise to make sound judgments about prisons and prisoners. Third, the courts were concerned that outside interference would subvert prison discipline.

The courts' actions, or lack of action, kept prison administrators free of external scrutiny except for financial accountability, and at the same time kept the court dockets from being cluttered with inmate suits. Due process ended at the front gate of the prison. Those who were incarcerated for crimes were believed to have forfeited their rights, or most of their rights, and there is little doubt that most citizens would have heartily agreed with the courts.

COURTS HAVE CHANGED

Today this has changed and the courts have become the primary instrument for correctional change. Through court action, inmates during these years have gained much broader freedoms in terms of religious practices, access to courts and counsel, correspondence and visitations. They have also won protection against cruel and unusual punishment, and recognition of their rights to orderly procedures for redress of grievances. More than 1,000 of these cases have been decided since 1960, and while inmate suits have not all been successful, it is

23

obvious that the traditional "hands-off" doctrine is dead and buried.

The courts have helped to introduce an era of more open and responsive government, and today no correctional administrator expects to be free of scrutiny by the courts, by the legislature, by the press and by the public.

FIRST U.S. COED PRISON OFFERS WIDE VARIETY OF PROGRAMS

The Federal Correctional Institution at Fort Worth is a minimum security facility for both men and women, the Bureau's first co-correctional institution.

Men and women 20 years and older are committed to Fort Worth either directly from the courts or as transfers from other institutions when they are within two years of release.

Education facilities offer individualized programs enabling inmates to work at their own pace from adult basic education through high school equivalency courses. There is an active study release program with Tarrant County Junior College, Texas Christian University, and the University of Texas at Arlington.

Vocational training is offered in television production and seven other fields. UNICOR (Federal Prison Industries) operates an automatic data processing center and a graphics shop employing up to 65 inmates.

Recreational activities include volleyball, baseball, basketball, and weightlifting.

Community involvement is encouraged. Furloughs, town trips, and work release are used to increase inmate involvement in special study, religious, and social groups. Alcoholics Anonymous and Toastmasters are active at the institution.

The Health Services Department has a medical/surgical clinic, hospital, and pharmacy and is staffed by three full-time doctors. The dental clinic is run by two full-time dentists and one dental assistant. There are also four staff psychologists.

A full-time Protestant minister and Catholic chaplain provide a wide variety of religious programs, counseling, and worship services.

Inmate complaints can no longer be summarily dismissed on the theory that their constitutional rights are suspended when they enter prison. The courts in extreme cases are willing to interfere in the management of prisons. They no longer believe that the day-to-day administration of institutions are the exclusive responsibility of the executive branch of government, and they have put the various legislatures on notice that while appropriating money for these institutions is primarily a legislative function, funding levels must be adequate to provide decent and humane conditions of incarceration. Ten states and the Federal system are under order to end overcrowding in their institutions.

COURTS PROMOTE PRISON PROGRESS

While as a correctional administrator I may quarrel with some individual court decisions, there is no question that on the whole the courts have demonstrated courage and wisdom in the rulings of the past few years. The courts have been responsible for much of the progress that has taken place in prisons, mental hospitals and other institutions over the past two decades.

Public administrators, whether running mental hospitals or prisons or similar facilities, have tended to regard the courts as adversaries. I believe this attitude is beginning to change as it becomes clear to us that the courts are in many instances our allies. No warden or correctional administrator wants an overcrowded institution or an institution that was built in the last century and whose antiquated character makes it impossible to provide inmates with humane living conditions.

Administrators can more readily carry out their responsibilities to provide secure and safe working and living conditions for both staff and inmates in the more modern prisons that are being built today.

While education, mental health, highway construction and other public services each has a powerful and vocal constituency to help secure needed resources, corrections has no such strong community support. We have no effective constituency. Consequently, the tendency is for funding bodies to put corrections at the bottom of the priority list.

The courts in recent years have moved to fill the vacuum created by the lack of a constituency for corrections. Federal and State courts alike are calling attention to unsatisfactory conditions in prisons and jails and are mandating that improvements be made.

Those of us involved in correctional administration have been at fault in not making correctional needs known in an effective fashion. We have tended to be insulated from the

25

mainstream of the political process. Our walls have kept the public out as well as kept the inmates in. We have neglected to adequately inform the public of our problems and consequently the community — and that includes the legal profession and the press — have not been fully aware of conditions in institutions. Fortunately this situation is changing as the courts have moved forward in expanding inmate rights and improving living conditions and as correctional administrators are coming to understand the value of opening institutions to the public, and what is more important, their duty to do so.

We were all caught by surprise by the tremendous influx of offenders into prisons over the past few years. Prisons and jails throughout the nation, almost without exception, have become overcrowded...

CAFETERIA AT COED PRISON IN FORT WORTH

Until five years ago, prison populations were stable on the Federal level and in most of the states. It was impossible to foresee the rapid rise in crime which has resulted in more offenders being apprehended and sentenced to a period of incarceration. Prison populations rose 25 percent during the 1975 and 1976 period alone. Since the time span to find a site for an institution, secure funding, design and build a new facility is about five years, it is understandable why institutions today are overcrowded.

To a large extent, the state and federal legislatures have gone a long way towards meeting correctional needs. Budgets have been increased and over the past few years, a great number of new community-based programs have been established. Programs such as furloughs and halfway houses and experimental programs such as restitution and pre-trial diversion have been developed. At the same time, the more traditional community-based programs of parole and probation have been enlarged and strengthened.

COMMUNITY BASED ALTERNATIVES

Today less than one-third of offenders under Federal supervision are in prison. The majority are in community-based alternatives to incarceration. In 1960, there were virtually no halfway houses in this country. Today, there are more than 1,000 such facilities serving offenders.

Without question the use of community alternatives should be maximized to the fullest extent possible, consistent with the public interest. They are less corrosive to offenders than institutions and are far less costly to the taxpayer. For those offenders who repeatedly commit crimes, particularly violent crimes, however, we will continue to need prisons.

During the past 20 years, the criminal justice system has been changed through law — law both in terms of new legislation and, more importantly, through the broadening of inmate rights by the courts. In no area has the expansion been as dramatic as in the area of the rights of prisoners. In the *Wolfe vs. McDonnell* case of 1974, the Supreme Court guaranteed prisoners due process in prison disciplinary hearings.

The courts have attempted — and I think for the most part successfully — to strike a new and fairer balance between the Constitutional guarantees for the individual and the legitimate interests of society as a whole. Obviously, offenders can't enjoy every right and privilege guaranteed to citizens in society. What the courts have done is to establish new rules of humaneness and fairness in the light of contemporary standards of society. The courts have brought the law and Constitutional guarantees firmly and decisively into our institutions and have done so in such a way that the safety of society is not endangered.

The courts have also made all of us more aware that we are responsible for the health, welfare and safety of individuals in custody. Offenders no longer surrender all their rights and no longer lose the protection of the law because their freedoms have been curtailed by the due process of society. We cannot expect offenders to learn to respect the law if they are subjected to lawlessness while confined.

CONCLUSIONS

Prisons and jails are slowly changing, and I believe for the better. Inmates have more rights than ever before and while progress is admittedly slow, institutions are being made more humane and safe. A wide variety of programs — including education, work, training and counseling — are becoming available. Community-based alternatives give the courts greater flexibility in dealing with offenders, and offenders themselves have more opportunities to help themselves make the decision to become law-abiding citizens.

Today the rule of law touches every citizen, as the founders of our country envisioned. We look forward to the day when every offender has a reasonable degree of privacy to protect his security and his humanity.

"You will have no 'rights,' so don't delude yourself into thinking that you do."

WHAT TO EXPECT IN PRISON

Winston Moseley

Winston Moseley has been a prisoner in the New York state prison system for many years. He writes frequently for *Fortune News*, published by Fortune Society. Fortune Society is an organization of ex-convicts and other persons interested in prison reform.

Winston Moseley, "34 Ways to Play A Loser's Game," *Fortune News*, October 1978. Reprinted with permission.

29

Crime is *a loser's game* for most, and just the appellation of the word *criminal* to you may well cause your family and friends untold anguish. Starting with the lead-in of arrest and into jail, then eventual plea-bargaining or trial, it's all downhill.

Errant individuals convicted of felonies and ticketed for prison ought to know that the following list of unpleasantries await them behind tall massive penitentiary walls.

1. First of all, expect to be stranded in prison for awhile, and maybe for many long, trying, lonesome years.

2. If you must be in prison for over three years, expect to lose contact with some or all of your family and former friends.

3. Don't expect anyone to agree with "your notion" of justice, nor will some miracle come along that will instantaneously affect your release.

4. Don't expect to soon if ever win a reversal from any higher court on appeal. The vast majority of imprisoned persons lose their appeals consistently.

5. There will be absolutely no privacy, and you can expect to do "hard time" in a hostile environment.

6. Don't expect the twisted circumstances of imprisonment in themselves to improve anyone's character or disposition. Since association is forced and limited by the very nature of the prison situation, some of your companions will oscillate between explosive bad temper and being boisterously annoying. Others will be unapproachably withdrawn to the point of being totally uncommunicative.

7. In prison you have been thrust into an abnormal twilight zone where neurosis, psychosis, and paranoia reign supreme. You are to be pitied if you need or expect any meaningful psychiatric help. Prison personnel won't take any special interest in you or your problems.

8. Expect no compassion, love, or sympathy from your fellow prisoners or from your keepers.

9. There will undoubtedly be overcrowding, continuous backbiting, and endless gossip out of which all kinds of wild rumors will come. What little fact and truth that is circulated around in prison is unfortunately mangled by most prisoners.

10. Expect the 6 x 8 cell that will be your home to be filthy. Your bed, graced with a dirty mattress, will be ancient,

and one or more of your fixtures, electricity (lights), sink or toilet, may not work.

11. You will wear prison issued ill-fitting perma-wrinkle clothing that will always be in short supply. The scuffed shoes you will be given may have been worn by ten men before you.

12. Every door (and there are many) will be securely locked, and the food will be terrible.

13. There is continual confusion in prison, loud discordant noises from morning to night, and often vermin — mice, rats, flies, mosquitoes, roaches and an abundance of other sundry insects.

14. There will be an interminable wait for anything and everything, and your incoming mail will be read before you get it no matter official claims to the contrary. Everyone in authority, administrators and guards, habitually lie to prisoners. Prisoners can also be expected to regularly lie.

THE BIG SQUEEZE

15. Little respect, honor or integrity is to be found in prison, but discourtesy and dishonesty inclusive of petty theft are commonplace occurrences.

16. Every imprisoned individual will have his own unique sad tale to tell, and most prisoners will at least make a claim of "technical innocence."

17. There are hundreds of written and unwritten rules that attempt to govern your in-prison behavior, but don't expect any practical everyday guidance. There is no set criteria, specific steps or programs for making parole, and no logical or reasonable explanations are going to be given for anything.

18. Monotony, regimentation—*sameness*—will characterize your existence, so you may expect to experience the depths of frustration.

19. You will be hustled, jostled, and manipulated from every conceivable angle, and you can expect half of the prisoners you meet to be armed with some kind of crude weapon.

20. Whimsical transfers from one prison to another are frequent; and there will be little or no association with the opposite sex.

21. Expect rampant homosexuality, guard and prisoner brutality (physical and psychological), vicious prison politics concentrated in the hands of a few concerned with the preservation of their own special privileges for the most part, and there will also be a plethora of non-political tight-knit cliques, none of which will welcome you.

22. Without going out of your way in the least, you can count on violating one or more of the prison's many rules and regulations. A punishment of some sort will surely follow.

23. Notes to the warden, counselors or other administrative personnel will be tersely answered in a condescending way in a matter of days — if you're lucky.

24. Where you perceive some unfairness or wrong and individually or collectively seek redress through petition via mail to any official in the Dept. of Correction in the state's capital, expect disappointment, a flat rejection of your allegations or contentions.

25. You will have no "rights," so don't delude yourself into thinking that you do.

26. You will hear guards and prisoners applying derogatory terms to all races and ethnic groups, there will be guard harassment, and in disputes between guard and prisoner, the prisoner invariably loses.

27. Forget about learning a trade or picking up a marketable skill. Jobs in prison, all of them lousy, are geared solely toward the maintenance of the prison system.

28. There will be days when you won't be able to get certain essentials, toothpaste, toilet paper, razor blades, and/or whatever official forms you may need for various purposes.

29. If you're fortunate, you will get two showers a week, *but*— in an unsanitary area where the water will always be too cold or too hot, and more likely than not, you won't be supplied with a washcloth or towel.

30. The sheets for your bed will often be torn or raggedy, and they will seldom match the size of your mattress.

31 Bacterial and viral epidemics periodically plague prisons, so expect to catch whatever is going around.

32. Don't expect the best in dental or medical care.

33. Expect prison clergy to sanction by silence, official and unofficial prison policy no matter how inhumane.

34. Don't be fooled into thinking that prison can be likened to a small harmonious community or society. There will be little or no unity of purpose, and your aims and goals probably won't coincide with those of anyone else.

Always warped to a greater or lesser degree, things are never quite as they appear to be in prison—but all to be seen or felt in penal institutions are variegated facets of bad situations impervious to improvement. If therefore, YOU would avoid a seared soul and hellish degradation, *don't play with crime's fire.*

> *"The act of rape in the ultra-masculine world of prison constitutes the ultimate humiliation visited upon a male,...the act redefines him as a 'female' in this reverse subculture and he must assume that role as the 'property' of his conqueror or whoever claimed him and arranged his demasculation. He becomes a slave in the fullest sense of the term."*

PRISON RAPE — THE STORY OF JAMES DUNN

This viewpoint was taken from *The Angolite*, the prison news-magazine of Louisiana State Penitentiary. It appeared in the November/December 1979 issue. It was written by inmates, as is all material in the newsmagazine.

Consider these questions while reading:
1. What do the authors mean when they say that "rape in prison is rarely a sexual act"?
2. What is meant by the inmate term "turning out"?
3. What did it mean for James Dunn to become another inmate's "old lady"?
4. What choices did James Dunn have in prison when confronted by a rapist?
5. What would you do if you were James Dunn?

THE STORY OF JAMES DUNN

James Dunn was one of the exceptions; he freed himself from his enslaved state, but at a terrible price. Dunn first came to Angola in March 1960 at the tender age of 19, toting a three-year sentence for burglary. A month after his arrival, he received a call to go to the Library, where an inmate "shoved me into a dark room where his partner was waiting. They beat me up and raped me. That was to claim me," Dunn explains. "When they finished, they told me that I was for them, then went out and told everyone else that they had claimed me." He recalls his reaction as being "one of fear, of wanting to survive. Once it happened, that was it—unless you killed one of them, and I was short and wanted to go home. So I decided I'd try to make the best of it." He cites as an influencing factor in his decision: "During my first week here, I saw 14 guys rape one youngster cause he refused to submit. They snatched him up, took him into the TV Room and, Man, they did everything to him—I mean, EVERYTHING, and they wouldn't even use no grease. When they finished with him, he had to be taken to the hospital where they had to sew him back up, then they had to take him to the nuthouse at Jackson cause he cracked up." Shaking his head at the memory, he says: "Man, I didn't want none of that kind of action, and my only protection was in sticking with my old man, the guy who raped me."

Few female rape victims in society must repay their rapist for the violence he inflicted upon them by devoting their existence to servicing his every need for years after—but rape victims in the world of prison must. And, Dunn, like the others, became his "old lady," his "wife." And, as his wife, he did "whatever the hell he wanted me to do." The alternative, Dunn points out was: "Back then, they'd throw acid in a kid's face, beat 'em up, and everything else you can think of." But Dunn was fortunate, in that all his owner required of him was for him to be a good housewife. And he was. He'd wash and take care of his old man's clothing, fix the beds, prepare meals, bust pimples in his face and give him massages, and generally do all of the menial things needed doing. As with all other wives around the world, he'd also take care of his man's sexual needs, with the only difference being that he could never say "no." His old man had a dope habit and once, while not having enough money to get a "fix," he sold Dunn in exchange for two bags of heroin and the settlement of a hundred dollar debt. As a slave, his market value at the time was $150. "Two weeks later," Dunn recounts, "he bought me back because he was loving me." Two months later, Dunn was paroled.

HOMOSEXUAL RAPE

Homosexual rapes can be kept at a minimum by diligent administration. Conjugal visits would certainly reduce the need of homosexual relations for some. The work release program could be expanded to include a periodic "home leave" for those who qualify. But these simple measures have been needed for a long time now, and there is no indication that they will be implemented in the near future.

Meanwhile, make certain that your young son doesn't get jammed up with the law and sent to this prison. For a carton of cigarettes, I can get him moved right into my cell, and I've been ten years without a woman.

There are many men like me in all of the prisons of the United States.

The author of the above statement is Mike Misenheimer. He is pictured on the left. His comments are taken from "Prison Sex", a chapter he wrote for the book *An Eye For An Eye.*

At the age of 21, Dunn returned to Angola for parole violation and a five-year sentence for burglary. His former owner was still here and "He let me know in no uncertain terms that things hadn't changed, that I was still his old lady," he says. "And he had a clique to back him up if I had any questions about it. Back then, cliques were running everything and that was how you survived.

Dunn did not rebel. He was eligible for parole again in two years and he didn't want to do anything that would mess up his chances of perhaps making it. But he had changed somewhat. While he went on and accepted the role of slave again, he was already thinking of ways to free himself of that state. "I waited on the parole, playing it cool, so that I wouldn't jeopardize it," he recalls, "but I made up my mind that if I missed the parole, I'd do something to stop this and become a man again, the kind of a man I could respect...I was being used. I was a slave. There was nothing I could do on my own. I had to have permission from my old man for everything I wanted to do, even to just step out of the dormitory, to go anywhere or do anything. Hell, my life wasn't mine—it was his, and I just lived for his pleasure. I didn't want to live like that. I was tired of it."

The Parole Board denied his request for a parole. "And I decided that I wasn't going to live that kind of life no longer," he says. "And when my old man went home, I had made up my mind that I wasn't gonna be for nobody else." He knew it wouldn't be easy and that he could be killed. "You know how it was back then, the attitude and all—once a whore, always a whore," he explains. "Everything and everybody in here worked to keep you a whore once you became one—even the prison. If a whore went to the authorities, all they'd do is tell you that since you were already a whore, they couldn't do nothing for you, and for you to go on back to the dorm and settle down and be a good old lady. Hell, they'd even call a whore's old man up and tell him to take you back down and keep you quiet. Now, if you wasn't a whore and you went to them, that was different — they'd take some action. But if you was already a whore, their attitude was more or less that you just go on and be one, and the most you'd get out of complaining is some marriage counseling, with them talking to you and your old man to iron out your difficulties. As for the courts, they didn't give a damn about prisoners back then and they wouldn't interfere in what happened up here. So, when I decided to quit being a whore, I knew that I would be bucking everything — prisoners, personnel, the whole damn system."

PRISON RAPE

Penal administrators rarely talk about the sexual violence that plague their institutions, turning them into literal jungles. Prisoners are too involved to ever want to do anything more than forget it once they regain their freedom. On the rare occasions the subject is discussed, it is mildly referred to as "the homosexual problem," as if it's a matter of individual sexual preference or perversion, something done only by homosexual "perverts," sickos slobbering at the mouth for an attractive young boy. And it's often the butt of jokes. But rape and sexual violence in prison has little to do with "heterosexuality" or "homosexuality" and is not the work of sexually-crazed perverts. And, despite the humerous references to it, it is a deadly serious affair in the pained world behind bars, almost always a matter of power and control and often, of life and death...

Rape in prison is rarely a sexual act, but one of violence, politics and an acting out of power roles. "Most of your homosexual rapes is a macho thing," says Col. Walter Pence, the Chief of Security here at the Louisiana State Penitentiary at Angola. "It's basically one guy saying to another: 'I'm a better man than you and I'm gonna turn you out to prove it.' I've investigated about a hundred cases personally, and I've not seen one that's just an act of passion. It's definitely a macho/power thing among the inmates. And it's the basically insecure prisoners who do it."

The act of rape in the ultramasculine world of prison constitutes the ultimate humiliation visited upon a male, the forcing of him to assume the role of a woman. It is not sexual and not really regarded as "rape" in the same sexual sense that society regards it. It is and means something entirely different in the world behind bars. In fact, it isn't even referred to as "rape." In the Louisiana penal system, both prisoners and personnel generally refer to the act as "turning out," a non-sexual description that reveals the non-sexual nature of what is really an act of conquest and demasculation, stripping the male-victim of his status of "man." The act redefines him as a "female" in this perverse subculture and he must assume that role as the "property" of his conqueror or whoever claimed him and arranged his demasculation. He becomes a slave, in the fullest sense of the term.

He told his old man how he felt and expressed the desire to be a man again. When his old man was freed from prison, probably because he cared for Dunn, instead of selling him or transferring his ownership of him to a friend, he left Dunn on his own. Without an old man, other inmates moved in on Dunn in attempts to claim him as their property. It wasn't difficult for him to find the determination to stick to his resolution to be a man. "After literally being screwed in and screwed over, misused and treated like an animal for so long, I had learned how to hate," he explains. So he fought. There were between fifteen to twenty fights during the next two months. But the strain and pressure he had to live under soon wore his nerves to a frazzle. "I was tired of this dumb shit. They wouldn't let me be a man, and I was tired of having to fight off everybody." His last fight was with Coyle Bell, an inmate serving time for kidnapping and rape. "He threatened me," Dunn says. "I did the only thing I could do. I killed him." That cost him an 18-months stay in a cell, but killing made a difference. "Nobody tried to claim me anymore," he recounts. "I was finally free—but it cost like hell." That killing added a life sentence to his original time, and, after 17 years here, he's still paying the price of his freedom from sexual enslavement.

For the next four years, his life was relatively peaceful, and he was his own man, belonging to no one. But this peaceful state of affairs only lasted until 1968 when he had to fight once more, an incident in which he stabbed another inmate. That added six more years to his sentence and got him a 13-month stay in a cell, a period that proved beneficial to him. "Man, I got to thinking that this was all so futile," he recalls. "I wanted to get out of prison, but I was just getting deeper and deeper into it. And it was there that I decided that, no matter what happened, I would do everything in my power to try to prevent what happened to me from happening to other kids." That became his personal mission in life, one he's pursued since. Upon his return to the Big Yard, Dunn went to work, waiting for the weekly new arrivals to the prison and pulling the youngsters over to the side and educating them on the various games of con and violence that other inmates would play on them in attempts to turn them out. If they needed money or items from the store, he would personally take them to the canteen and buy whatever they needed so as to prevent their borrowing things from guys who would later insist upon collecting their debt by turning them out. A substantial number of youngsters have been helped over the years by Dunn, taking them by the hand and personally leading them through the thicket of games and intrigues played by inmates to snare the unlearned and unwary into a cobweb of violence and slavery. Doing something to help and protect the young and the weak has

DISTINGUISHING BETWEEN FACT AND OPINION

This discussion exercise is designed to promote experimentation with one's ability to distinguish between fact and opinion. It is a fact, for example, that the United States was militarily involved in the Vietnam War. But to say this involvement served the interests of world peace is an opinion or conclusion. Future historians will agree that American soldiers fought in Vietnam, but their interpretations about the causes and consequences of the war will probably vary greatly.

PART I

Instructions

Some of the following statements are taken from this book and some have other origins. Consider each statement carefully. Mark *O* for any statement you feel is an opinion or interpretation of the facts. Mark *F* for any statement you believe is a fact. Then discuss and compare your judgments with those of other class members.

O = OPINION
F = FACT

_____ 1. The pay scales of prison officers are generally so low that they cannot attract personnel with adequate background to work effectively with inmates.

_____ 2. Federal prisons are developing more effective rehabilitation programs.

_____ 3. The courts have become the primary instrument for correctional change.

_____ 4. The most fertile ground for the cultivation of criminals is the prison system itself.

_____ 5. The mollycoddling of vicious criminals by our courts and prisons has helped to raise the crime rate.

_____ 6. Punishment does not deter crime and, therefore, should not be part of any prison sentence.

_____ 7. Capital punishment clearly violates the basic Christian principles of love and forgiveness.

_____ 8. Prison rapes can be kept at a minimum by diligent administration.

_____ 9. Prisons serve no useful purpose.

_____ 10. More federal prison inmates are imprisoned for robbery than counterfeiting.

_____ 11. Corporal punishment practiced in some Eastern cultures is more barbaric than our custom of imprisonment.

_____ 12. Rehabilitation can cure and reform criminal tendencies.

PART II

Instructions

STEP 1
The class should break into groups of four to six students.

STEP 2
Each small group should try to locate two statements of fact and two statements of opinion in the book.

STEP 3
Each group should choose a student to record its statements.

STEP 4
The class should discuss and compare the small groups' statements.

Chapter **2**

AMERICA'S PRISONS

What is the Purpose of Prisons?

"Prisons are not known to serve any useful purposes...the abolition of prisons, on the other hand, will clearly stimulate experimentation in other methods of preventing crime."

PRISONS SERVE NO USEFUL PURPOSE

David F. Greenberg

David F. Greenberg was one of the principal authors of the American Friends Service Committee's report, *Struggle for Justice.* He is now Assistant Professor of Sociology at New York University.

Consider the following questions while reading:

1. According to Greenberg, what four functions does the public believe prisons serve in society?
2. According to him, how successful are prisons in carrying out these functions?
3. How does the author feel about the function of punishment in prisons?
4. What does the author suggest in place of prisons? Do you agree?

David F. Greenberg, *The Problems of Prisons*, 1970, pp. 1-31. (Published as an educational service by the NATIONAL PEACE LITERATURE SERVICE, American Friends Service Committee, 160 North 15th Street, Philadelphia, Pennsylvania.

44

One of the most difficult and one of the most ignored of our social problems is the problem of prisons — a problem which might be ameliorated through drastic prison reform, but which can be solved only through the abolition of prisons.

The elimination of imprisonment may at first seem like a radical step, but alternatives to imprisonment are already widespread — fines and probation are often used, and traffic law violators are sometimes sentenced to attend classes in driver education. The advocacy of prison abolition implies simply that other courses of action, including, sometimes, doing nothing at all, are preferable to imprisonment...

Most people believe that prisons exist to protect the public from those who commit anti-social acts, such as murder, rape, assault and theft. Another commonly accepted rationale for prisons is that they deter potential criminals...

A third role, the most ancient in origin, is that of punishment...

By contrast, modern day penologists and prison administrators, at least at the level of rhetoric, consider the most important function of a prison to be rehabilitation, the improvement of a defective individual so that he can return to society as an acceptably functioning member...

An important function of prisons is helping the public to avoid facing certain unpleasant problems...

It is nevertheless widely believed that prisons at least protect us from lower class criminals, thereby performing a useful and even necessary function...To carry the argument to completion, it remains to examine the relevance of prisons to the various functions listed earlier: protection, deterrence, punishment and rehabilitation...

PROTECTION

Almost all prisoners will sooner or later be released from prison, usually within a few years of incarceration, and regardless of any changes in the personality of the prisoner. Many prisoners are in fact released despite virtual certainty that they will soon return to prison. On a long term basis, then, prisons provide no protection...

On a short term basis, prisons may protect those outside their walls, but under anything like present conditions, they are unable to protect inmates from the crimes that flourish within their walls...

**PRISON ISN'T A WASTE OF TIME.
A LOT OF KIDS COME OUT LEARNING A TRADE.**

DETERRENCE

We *do* know that imprisonment is remarkably ineffective in deterring prison inmates from returning to crime after their release. Recidivism rates depend somewhat on the type of institution and the type of offender, and figures quoted are not always reliable, but figures of 60 to 85 per cent are commonly accepted...

PUNISHMENT

The notion that punishment by itself might *improve* the prisoner is even more curious than the notion that it might deter him from breaking laws in the future...

In a moral sense, the propriety of punishment at the hands of the state seems especially questionable. A government responsible for the murder of thousands or millions in war is not in a very good position to pass judgment on domestic killers, whose body count has no hope, in a lifetime, of matching what the state frequently accomplishes in a day or week. The overwhelming majority of murders committed in this century have been committed legally, by governments in wartime. The largest thefts in our country have been thefts of land guaranteed by treaty to Indian tribes and Chicanos in the Southwest — thefts sponsored by our government. The largest number of kidnappings — those of Japanese-Americans during World War II — were carried out by the government with approval of the courts.

REHABILITATION

We come now to the topic of rehabilitation — a word that can cover a multitude of sins and serves as the source of a good deal of bitterness to prisoners: despite much talk and slick government brochures (often printed in prison print shops) about rehabilitative programs, very few such programs can be found inside most prisons. Rehabilitation is still regarded as a luxury, something to think about after security and maintenance are insured. As a result, neither adequate funds nor staff is available for rehabilitation or treatment programs in most prisons...

Vocational training and educational programs, if upgraded, could be valuable to those whose primary motivation for crime was economic; but this training need not take place in prison, as is recognized by those few institutions making use, on a very limited basis, of work release programs. There is no need to put a person in jail before training him for a job. In fact, it seems somewhat irrational to provide job training only to those who have first committed a crime. The time for education and vocational training is *before* a crime has been committed...

"LAZY, YES SIR, BUT SHE'S VERY PRODUCTIVE!"

If we rule out purely retributive punishment as pointless, our survey of the functions that prisons are supposed to serve leads to the conclusion that prisons are not known to serve any useful purposes. The vocational, educational and psychological programs are largely undermined by the precedence given to security and maintenance of the institution, and could be operated much more successfully for those who want them, outside of prison, and on a voluntary basis. Since such programs would also be open to those who have not yet committed any crimes, this could also become a major contribution toward crime prevention. At the same time it will be necessary to eliminate the economic factors that lead to crime. In the long run, reorganization of society could eliminate much of the crime we see today. Probably no social reorganization will ever succeed in wiping out all manifestations of anti-social behavior, but this need not be a serious problem, even if alternatives to imprisonment are not found. A society that is prepared to tolerate 56,000 traffic fatalities a year has no reason to be worried about occasional murders; a society that squanders many billions a year on armaments is not really worried about petty theft, it only thinks it is.

Imprisonment is not very effective in deterring those who commit crime, and there is not much reason to believe that it deters those who have not yet done so. In particular, there is no reason to believe that different kinds of penalties, whether monetary or other, are less effective than imprisonment in obtaining adherence to laws. The use of rewards, such as cash incentives to prevent recidivism, remains wholly unexplored. We are not likely to know more about this as long as we can rely on prisons. The abolition of prisons, on the other hand, will clearly stimulate experimentation in other methods of preventing crime.

"The Bureau of Prison's philosophy attempts to maintain a balance among punishment, deterrence, incapacitation, and rehabilitation as purposes of incarceration."

THE PURPOSE OF FEDERAL PRISONS

Norman A. Carlson

Norman Carlson is the Director of the Bureau of Prisons of the U.S. He made the following statement before the Committee on the Judiciary Subcommittee on Penitentiaries and Corrections on June 29, 1978.

Consider these questions while reading:
1. **When was the Federal Bureau of Prisons established?**
2. **What are the purposes of incarceration, according to the Bureau of Prisons?**
3. **What did Dean Norval Morris have to say about rehabilitation programs which influenced the Bureau's philosophy?**

I would like to briefly discuss the history of the Federal Prison System. In 1929 a Congressional Committee was established to investigate conditions in the existing Federal prisons. At that time, there were seven institutions, housing 12,000 offenders, each funded separately by Congress and operated autonomously under policies and regulations established by the individual wardens. As a result of the Committee's report, Congress established the Federal Bureau of Prisons in the Department of Justice on May 14, 1930. The Congressional mandate was "to develop an integrated system of institutions and to provide custody and treatment based upon the individual needs of offenders."

The Federal Bureau of Prisons has grown substantially over the past 48 years, expanding from seven to thirty-eight institutions, ranging from maximum security penitentiaries to minimum security camps. In addition, there are 11 Community Treatment Centers (halfway houses) which are community-based facilities established in 1960 to ease the transition of inmates back into the community at the time of release. The Bureau also contracts with private agencies and State and local authorities for Community Treatment Center services.

During the decades of the 1950's and 1960's correctional philosophy in the United States developed into a system based on the concepts of classification and social casework. Through the proper classification of inmates, institutional administrators hoped to better manage their populations. Social and psychological casework complemented the classification process by providing individual treatment to offenders through education, religious, vocational training, and counseling programs in order to resolve their personal and social problems. The "medical model" of diagnosis, prescription and treatment evolved.

The Bureau of Prisons began its first major long-range planning effort in 1970. This resulted in a Master Plan that embraced the "medical model" concept in its long range goals and objectives. The plan identified two critical issues that remain important today: the reduction of overcrowding and the closing of the three antiquated penitentiaries at McNeil Island, Washington; Leavenworth, Kansas; and Atlanta, Georgia.

The medical treatment model was used in the development of a 10-year construction program. The Master Plan identified an eventual need for 66 additional institutions. Of these, 31 would be minimum custody institutions located in large metropolitan areas. They would have capacities of 150. This construction plan proved to be unworkable as the Bureau came to realize that communities would generally not allow these

BUREAU OF PRISONS

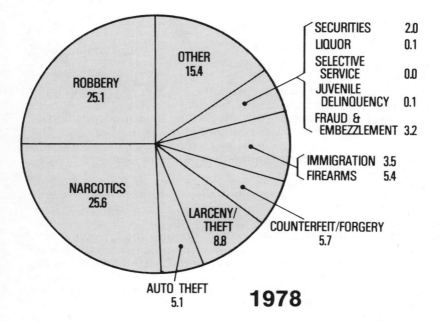

SECURITIES 2.0
LIQUOR 0.1
SELECTIVE SERVICE 0.0
JUVENILE DELINQUENCY 0.1
FRAUD & EMBEZZLEMENT 3.2
IMMIGRATION 3.5
FIREARMS 5.4
COUNTERFEIT/FORGERY 5.7

OTHER 15.4
ROBBERY 25.1
NARCOTICS 25.6
LARCENY/THEFT 8.8
AUTO THEFT 5.1

1978

THE PERCENTAGE OF POPULATION CONFINED TO INSTITUTIONS BY OFFENSE

Source: U.S. Department of Justice

facilities within their neighborhoods. In addition, the costs proved to be prohibitive.

The medical model of corrections began to be questioned in the mid-1970's. A highly influential report by Dr. Robert Martinson of the City University of New York in 1974 raised serious doubts about the ability of corrections to rehabilitate.

During this period the Bureau of Prisons, along with most correctional agencies, shifted its program philosophy from the medical treatment model to one that emphasized individual responsibility for program participation. The foremost catalyst for this change were the views of Dean Norval Morris, of the University of Chicago Law School. In his book, *The Future of Imprisonment*, Dean Morris argues that offenders should be incarcerated for what they have done, not for who they are. He indicates that inmate program participation must be voluntary if programs are to have any impact in changing behavior.

The Bureau of Prison's philosophy attempts to maintain a balance among punishment, deterrence, incapacitation, and rehabilitation as purposes of incarceration. Offenders are deprived of their liberty by the courts as punishment. During incarceration offenders are prevented from committing further crimes and such confinement serves to deter others. While incarcerated, they should be provided with programs and opportunities to change.

The construction program that was outlined in the 1970 Bureau of Prisons' Master Plan was altered to reflect the new philosophy. The long-range plan identified the need for fewer institutions. They would be small in comparison to older prisons with capacities limited to 500. It was believed that this was the optimum size to maintain operational efficiency and yet, at the same time, be small enough to provide adequate staff/inmate interaction. Moreover, they would be constructed as close as possible to large metropolitan areas to take advantage of community resources and encourage family visitation.

ALTERNATIVES TO INCARCERATION

The expanding use of alternatives to incarceration has significantly influenced the Bureau's long range construction program. Alternatives are less costly and less corrosive than imprisonment. During the past 10 years the use of alternatives in the Federal Criminal Justice System has been greatly expanded. At the prosecution level, United States Attorneys and the U.S. Probation System are involved in pre-trial diversion programs. When imposing sentences, Federal Courts make wide use of alternatives to incarceration. Of the 96,500

FEDERAL CORRECTIONAL SYSTEM

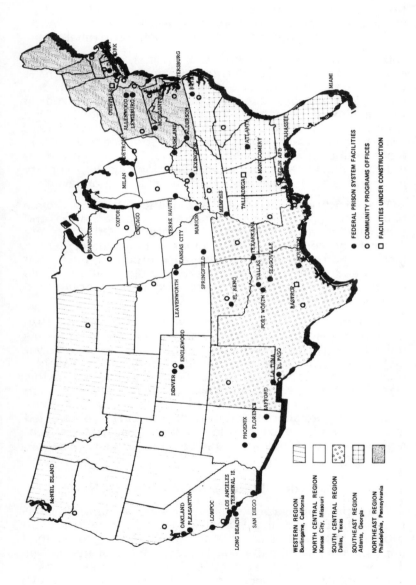

Source: U.S. Department of Justice

54

offenders currently under Federal supervision, less than one-third are incarcerated while the remainder are on probation or are involved in other community programs. Federal judges generally limit the use of incarceration to the most serious and chronic offenders.

The Community Treatment Center program has served as an alternative to new construction. Under the auspices of former Attorney General Robert F. Kennedy, the Federal Prison System initiated a halfway house program in the early 1960's. This was to be the first government operated halfway house (later to become known as Community Treatment Centers) program in the United States. Since that time, the program has expanded considerably. The program now utilizes both Federally operated Community Treatment Centers (CTC's) and State, local and private contracts. The Bureau uses the CTC program as a transitional program for offenders moving from institutions to release to the community. In addition to assisting offenders during this critical transitional period, the programs help to relieve overcrowding in institutions.

These programs also provide the Federal judiciary with another sentencing alternative. A Federal judge may sentence an offender to a term of probation with a condition that a portion of the term be spent in a CTC rather than a traditional institution.

The Bureau has also pursued other alternatives to the construction of correctional institutions. For many years we have contracted with State and local institutions to house Federal offenders. However, this alternative has been severely limited in recent years because of the high level of overcrowding in virtually every state prison system.

We plan to expand the use of both satellite camps and independent minimum security camps. Such camps are a less restrictive and less costly form of incarceration. Recent analysis indicates that up to 35 percent of the committed population could be housed in minimum custody facilities compared to 25 percent at the present time. We are currently constructing or expanding satellite camps at four institutions. In addition, negotiations have been ongoing with the Department of Defense to find appropriate sites to establish independent camps. Potential sites are currently being investigated at de-activated military bases at Boron, California and Big Spring, Texas.

The Bureau will continue to pursue alternatives to new construction that are consistent with the public interest and sound correctional management.

"The primary goal of a prison system is to take out of circulation those anti-social individuals who have murdered, raped, robbed, or committed other forms of criminal activity."

U.S. NEEDS MORE AND BETTER PRISONS

Allan C. Brownfeld

Allan Brownfeld writes a weekly column for *Roll Call*, the newspaper of the U.S. Congress. He is a recipient of the Wall Street Journal Foundation Award and has contributed to a number of magazines and journals.

Consider the following questions while reading:
1. **According to the author, what are the major causes of violence in prisons?**
2. **What does the author claim is ACLU's solution to prison problems?**
3. **What does it mean to be sent to prison *as* punishment, not *for* punishment.**
4. **What does the author say are three things which could contribute most to better prisons?**

Allan C. Brownfeld, "U.S. Needs More and Better Prisons," *Human Events*, April 12, 1980. Reprinted with the author's permission.

In the early February riot which occurred at the New Mexico State Penitentiary, 33 inmates were killed. The prison was almost destroyed. Prison Warden Jerry Griffin stated, "Man's inhumanity to man is mind-boggling."

The New Mexico riot, one of the worst in U.S. history, is viewed by experts as a case study in what is wrong with U.S. prisons — underfunded, understaffed, filled beyond capacity, seething with racial tension. In fact, a University of Alabama psychologist, an expert in prison work, wrote an article for the journal *Law and Human Behavior*, using the New Mexico penitentiary as an example of the effects of such conditions.

New Mexico's prison is hardly the worst. In half of our states, prisons house more inmates than they were built to hold. Although public officials tend to downplay it, the nation is in the grip of a mounting crime wave. As a result, the inmate population is growing. In the last five years, it jumped from 204,000 to nearly 300,000 — an increase of almost 40 per cent. Yet the space available for confining criminals has lagged far behind.

Overcrowding, for example, helped trigger a riot at the Georgia State Prison at Reidsville where one guard and two inmates were stabbed to death. Built to house 1,100 prisoners, the Georgia institution now holds nearly 2,500. Another riot occurred at the prison in Pontiac, Mich., constructed in 1871 to hold 600 prisoners — but now housing 2,000.

There has been almost a total breakdown of order within the nation's prisons. Nearly 100 inmates and guards have been killed in prisons in California alone since 1970. At the Michigan State Prison in Jackson, the world's largest, there have been seven murders in 18 months. In the last 10 years, 30 inmates have been killed at Walpole Prison in Massachusetts.

Those who oppose the very idea of prisons — even for dangerous criminals — are using the sad state of today's prison system as a basis for calling for an end to incarceration and the replacement of prisons with such "alternatives" as community correction centers, halfway houses, and a variety of work-release programs. The American Civil Liberties Union Prison Project is in the forefront of that crusade.

As a result of a lawsuit brought by the ACLU, U.S. Judge Frank Johnson declared in 1976 that the Alabama State Prison system was "unconstitutional." He said that conditions were so inhuman that they violated the 8th Amendment prohibition against cruel and unusual punishment. Among other things, the judge found "as many as six inmates were packed in 4-foot

57

by 8-foot cells with no beds, no lights, no running water, and a hole in the floor for a toilet."

A prison-rights lawyer, Daniel Steinbock, asked: "Would we tolerate a penal law that said guilty men must be sent away, gang raped and returned home? No, but we allow it to exist in fact."

In New Mexico, the brutality involved in the riot was extreme. Inmates shoved steel poles through each other's heads, held torches to their eyes, and hurled wounded bodies off second-story tiers. A former inmate, who spent 13 years in the New Mexico prison on a murder conviction, said: "They don't respect anything or anyone. When you have absolutely nothing left but your life, and it's worthless, you're capable of anything."

Americans face a situation in which the streets of our cities — and, now, even our small towns — are increasingly unsafe. In New York, for the first time in history, there were more than 1,700 murders in a single year — 1979. Albuquerque, N.M., had a crime increase of 20 per cent. Rather than following the advice of the ACLU and keeping criminals on the streets, it is just such leniency which has produced our current perilous situation. A 1978 New York study found that 70 per cent of those who had been arrested for homicide the previous year had been arrested at least once before for some crime.

In his book *Punishing Criminals*, Dr. Ernest van den Haag writes: "Punishment — if not the only, or the first, or even the best means of making people obey laws — is ultimately indispensable." Deprivation of freedom, Van den Haag argues, is the appropriate punishment for those who have violated the social compact with the greatest impunity. But violators are to be sent to prison *as* punishment, not *for* punishment. The conditions of imprisonment, he writes, should not, of themselves, conduce a worse criminal behavior.

Government officials who are unwilling to take the steps necessary to improve our prison facilities simply play into the hands of those who believe that, somehow, prison itself — however good the conditions — is anathema to a democratic society. "Rehabilitation" has, most experts now agree, largely failed. The primary goal of a prison system is to take out of circulation those anti-social individuals who have murdered, raped, robbed, or committed other forms of criminal activity.

"What are needed," the Washington *Star* declared, "are more prisons, and especially smaller prisons, better-trained and better-paid correctional personnel, more predictable sentencing. This does not imply a 'freer' or less restrictive prison regimen; indeed, it argues for the contrary — prisons run with

THE CRIMINAL ETHIC

On February 2, 1980 the New Mexico state prison was torn to pieces by a bloody riot. It stands alone in the annals of prison riots because of its wanton violence and utter lawlessness. A total of 33 inmates were killed in the riot, many of whom were brutally tortured and mutilated. As many as 200 other inmates were beaten and raped...

Some prisoners and a few of the more out-of-touch reformists will attribute the New Mexico violence to bad food, overcrowded living conditions, and lack of proper medical care. Those conditions may have precipitated the initial takeover, but no set of conditions justifies the bloodletting that followed. The bitter truth of the matter is that cliques of hardcore criminals took over the prison; those who have the criminal ethic buried in their brain. They know nothing else in life except the perverse values which governs their criminal lives. They know only how to take, pillage, and harm in the name of those values. They're incapable of respecting another man's right to live in peace because they are criminal.

Some of us have lived among the criminal ethic most of our lives. We know it because we've seen it express itself in the double-crossing drug killings in the free world, in the midnight prison killings where an old man is stabbed to death in his sleep, and in the gang-rapes of the youngsters who pass through the nation's jails. We also know that damn near everybody in prison tell on each other and work diligently to find the most devious ways of screwing the next man. That's a rooted part of the criminal ethic. We know we don't respect each other, and, in fact, we hate each other's guts. We're a damned class of people dedicated only to lies, deceit, treachery and the rip-off mentality. We must live in this abnormal prison subculture because we've been kicked out of the normal free world culture behind our criminal behavior. And can you blame the Man? Hell no. Not when we commit crimes of killing innocent persons because they won't cooperate with our robberies or because they didn't have enough money on them when we tried to rob them. Prison is necessary to protect the normal culture from that abnormal lawless behavior — and as long as we perpetuate an ethic which justifies that kind of behavior, the necessity of prison cannot be questioned.

From an inmate editorial in The Angolite, May-June 1980. *The Angolite* is the prison newsmagazine of Louisiana State Penitentiary.

---

stricter regulations even-handedly administered, and protection of inmates from the thugs who to a great extent determine life within the prison jungles today and impose their perverted values."

If we cannot keep our prisons safe and orderly, how can we hope to restore safety and security to our larger society?

VIEWPOINT 4

"Today, I think, most would agree that the prevailing correctional philosophy is moving back from a point at one extreme of the continuum to a position closer to the center. We once again recognize that offenders are sentenced by the courts for several reasons."

WE NEED A BALANCE IN CORRECTIONS

Norman A. Carlson

Normal Carlson is the Director of the U.S. Bureau of Prisons. He made the following statement before the American Correctional Association in Philadelphia on August 20, 1979.

Consider the following questions while reading:
1. What correctional philosophy was popular during the 1950's and 1960's, according to the author?
2. What philosophy was popular during the 1970's?
3. What does the author think the current correctional philosophy is?
4. What does the author see as major problems we face today in corrections?

The pendulum moves in corrections just as it does in every aspect of society, shifting from one point on a continuum to the other and eventually coming back toward the center. Such swings are not necessarily bad, as some would imply. Society needs change if it is to move forward. Nothing can be learned without innovation. As the noted sociologist Pitirim Sorokin indicates, movements of the pendulum are not only inevitable, they are desirable. Whatever the eventual outcome, each swing tends to produce a degree of lasting progress.

When describing previous correctional philosophies, the word "faddish" is frequently used. All too often, whenever a new idea appeared on the horizon, it was eagerly accepted and soon became the standard by which progress was measured.

If a particular program appeared to be effective in one context, the tendency was to move to the extreme position that it would, therefore, work in all situations. An example that comes to mind is group counseling — a program that, without question; has merit for some offenders in some situations. Following the successful introduction of group counseling programs in several institutions, the concept literally swept the correctional spectrum during the 1950's and early 1960's. Nearly every major institution in the country, as well as many probation and parole offices, introduced group counseling programs on a massive scale. The word was out. At long last corrections had found the solution — group counseling was the answer. A more recent example is the public fascination with the phenomenon, "Scared Straight".

As the result of frequent shifts in direction, the public has become understandably confused concerning the purposes and objectives of corrections. There appears to be no central theme or consistent philosophy being pursued. What was considered yesterday's major objective is no longer held valid today.

When speaking of balance, we are referring to a mid point on a continuum. In corrections, there are many forces involved and, hence, the task of achieving balance is difficult. The various factors to be balanced include:
• Society's concern with protection *and* the needs of offenders.
• The constitutional rights of offenders *and* the requirement for order and discipline.
• Punishment *and* treatment.
• The apparently inconsistent objectives of retribution, deterrence, incapacitation *and* rehabilitation.

During the past decade, we have seen the most recent major swing in philosophy. Recognizing that simply punishing offenders was not the answer, corrections turned increasingly to the social and behavioral sciences. The disciplines of social work, psychology and psychiatry were introduced into the correctional process. The oft criticized "medical model" evolved — the concept that offenders were somehow sick and could be successfully diagnosed and treated, regardless of motivation or desire. A new lexicon developed — treatment modalities, diagnostic summaries, and therapeutic intervention.

The hope was that by treating offenders, we could successfully intervene in their lifestyles and, thereby, reduce recidivism. Subsequent research unfortunately has failed to substantiate these hopes. Studies completed both in this country as well as abroad indicate how little we know about changing human behavior.

NATIONAL INSTITUTE OF CORRECTIONS

The Federal Bureau of Prisons acquired major new responsibilities during Fiscal Year 1975.

The National Institute of Corrections was created by Congress and lodged in the Bureau of Prisons to help local and state corrections agencies upgrade and improve their operations.

The Bureau moved to establish a more balanced system of corrections, one that recognizes that retribution, deterrence and rehabilitation are all important elements in the criminal justice system.

From *Sandstone*, an undated publication by the Department of Justice and printed by inmates at the Federal Correctional Institution, Sandstone, Minnesota.

One universal characteristic of human nature is to search for easy answers to complex issues. This is particularly true in respect to corrections. The nature of our task requires that we avoid seeking simplistic solutions to the problems of crime and delinquency. No single approach is appropriate for all offenders, nor will any magic change satisfy all our critics. On one point we all can agree, there are no panaceas — nor will there be.

Many of you will recall Norval Morris' provocative keynote address at the 1975 Congress of Corrections in Louisville. In that speech, Dean Morris commented, with obvious tongue in cheek, that crime could be significantly reduced — by simply locking up all males until they are 40 years old. Years earlier, the noted philosopher, H.L. Mencken, put it another way when he stated that for every complex social problem there was a solution — *easy*, *simple*, and *wrong*!

Today, I think most would agree that the prevailing correctional philosophy is moving back from a point at one extreme of the continuum to a position closer to the center. We once again recognize that offenders are sentenced by the courts for several reasons:

- As punishment for their crimes.
- To incapacitate them from committing further criminal acts.
- To deter both themselves and others.
- And, to provide them opportunities to change their lifestyles.

In acknowledging this shift of the pendulum, we are not saying, as some would imply, that corrections is moving to the other extreme on the continuum where punishment alone is the answer. What we *are* doing is recognizing that man cannot change his fellow man — unless that person wants to change.

I believe the courts are also moving toward a more balanced position in respect to corrections. During the most recent term, the U.S. Supreme Court handed down three important opinions, two relating to parole, and the other to institutions. In all three cases, the Court recognized the need to balance the rights of offenders with the legitimate interests of society.

Contrary to what some have suggested, the courts are not returning to the "hands off" doctrine of the past. Careful reading of these and other decisions clearly indicates that courts will continue to exercise their full authority whenever the constitutional rights of offenders are violated. At the same time, the courts are recognizing the difficult challenges we face in carrying out our statutory responsibilities to protect society...

Today, we face a series of major problems. The number of inmates confined in prisons and jails has skyrocketed by over 50 percent during the past seven years. Caseloads in most probation and parole offices are far above accepted standards for effective supervision. Communities are increasingly unwilling to accept halfway houses and similar programs. More importantly, corrections, like other governmental programs, is experiencing a decline in budgetary support as a result of the "taxpayer revolt".

Despite this note of pessimism, we must continue to push forward...

None of us can be satisfied with unmanageable caseloads, overcrowded institutions, or severely limited alternatives to incarceration. We cannot be content with inmate idleness, antiquated facilities, or inadequate staffing patterns.

Ways must be found to return to society individuals who at least are no worse than they were when initially committed to our supervision.

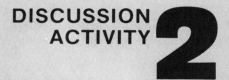

DISTINGUISHING PRIMARY FROM SECONDARY SOURCES

A critical thinker must always question his various sources of information. Historians, for example, usually distinguish between *primary sources* (eyewitness accounts) and *secondary sources* (writings based on primary or eyewitness accounts, or other secondary sources.) A diary written by a Civil War veteran is one example of a primary source. In order to be a critical reader one must be able to recognize primary sources. However, this is not enough. Eyewitness accounts do not always provide accurate descriptions. Historians may find ten different eyewitness accounts of an event and all the accounts might interpret the event differently. Then they must decide which of these accounts provide the most objective and accurate interpretations.

PART I

Instructions

Pretend you are living 500 years in the future. Your teacher tells you to write an essay about crime and prisons in America between the years of 1970 and 1980. Consider carefully each of the following source descriptions. Assume they all deal with crime and prisons in America.

65

STEP 1

First, underline only those descriptions you feel would serve as a primary source for your essay.

STEP 2

Second, rank only the underlined or primary sources. Assign the number 1 to the most objective and accurate primary source. Assign the number 2 to the next most accurate source and so on until the ranking is finished.

_____ 1. A book by a prison warden written in 1974

_____ 2. An essay by a prison inmate written in 1978

_____ 3. A 1975 television interview with a white policeman working in an all white suburb

_____ 4. A 1975 essay by a white policeman working in Harlem

_____ 5. A 1975 newspaper editorial by a black policeman working in Harlem

_____ 6. A book by Norman A. Carlson, the Director of the Federal Bureau of Prisons, written in 1979

_____ 7. The viewpoint in this book by Clarence Billingsley, prison inmate

_____ 8. A book by Martin Luther King written in 1967

_____ 9. A 1977 newspaper editorial by a Chicago banker

_____ 10. The viewpoint in this book by Alan F. Kay

_____ 11. An essay by Senator Edward Kennedy written in 1984

_____ 12. An essay by an American sociologist written in 1966

_____ 13. A book by President Ford written in 1975

_____ 14. An article by Fidel Castro written in 1978

_____ 15. A book by Richard Nixon written in 1978

_____ 16. An essay by a Japanese journalist written in 1973

PART II

Instructions

All class members should discuss and compare each individual's rankings. Individuals should be able to defend their rankings.

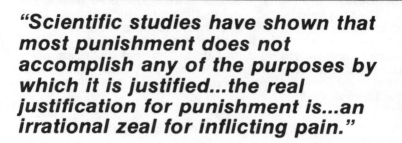

"Scientific studies have shown that most punishment does not accomplish any of the purposes by which it is justified...the real justification for punishment is...an irrational zeal for inflicting pain."

THE CRIME OF PUNISHMENT

Karl Menninger

Dr. Menninger was a founder of the Menninger School of Psychiatry. He is also a founder or charter member of several other psychiatric associations, including the Kansas Psychiatric Society and the American Orthopsychiatric Association. He holds six professorships in psychiatry in various university medical schools. He has written about a dozen books. His most recent book *Whatever Became of Sin?* was published in 1973.

Consider the following questions while reading:
1. *Why does the author oppose punishment? What are some of his specific arguments?*
2. *What distinction does he make between penalties and punishment?*
3. *How does Menninger relate today's public attitude toward criminals and the attitude toward mental illness a hundred years ago?*

The law, like a large part of the body politic, assumes that punishment is a proper thing for the proper persons. It is an axiom that one who breaks the rules must be punished. Whether this punishment does him any good or not, whether it actually deters him or others from further actions of the same sort whether indeed it does not cost more than other forms of deterrence — all such questions are considered beside the point, in law as in public opinion. Scientific studies have shown that most punishment does not accomplish any of the purposes by which it is justified, but neither the law nor the public cares anything about that. The real justification for punishment is none of these rational "purposes," but an irrational zeal for inflicting pain upon one who has inflicted pain (or harm or loss)...

PENALTIES, NOT PUNISHMENT

Is it true, I am asked, that you oppose *all* punishment for *everyone*? Think of some of the fiendish crimes that we all hear about from time to time. Do you think such persons should go unpunished? You seem to favor penalties; how do they differ from punishments?

Certainly the abolition of punishment does not mean the omission or curtailment of penalties; quite the contrary. Penalties should be greater and surer and quicker in coming. I favor stricter penalties for many offenses, and more swift and certain assessment of them.

But these are not *punishments* in the sense of long-continued torture — pain inflicted over years for the sake of inflicting pain. If I drive through a red light, I will be and should be penalized. If a bridge player overbids, he is promptly and surely penalized, and his opponents can even double the penalty. If he cheats, he may be excluded from the game, but no one beats him or locks him up...

I do not think this means that we psychiatrists are too senti-mental. Being against punishment is not a sentimental conviction. It is a logical conclusion drawn from scientific experi-ence. It is also a professional principle; we doctors try to relieve pain, not cause it...

The present penal system and the existing legal philosophy do not stimulate or even expect...a change to take place in the criminal. Yet change is what medical science always aims for. The prisoner, like the doctor's other patients, should emerge from his treatment experience a different person, differently equipped, differently functioning, and headed in a different direction from when he began the treatment.

CRIMINALS CAN CHANGE

It is natural for the public to doubt that this can be accomplished with criminals. But remember that the public *used* to doubt that change could be effected in the mentally ill. Like criminals, the mentally ill were only a few decades ago regarded as definitely unchangeable — "incurable." No one a hundred years ago believed mental illness to be curable: Today *all* people know (or should know) that *mental illness is curable* in the great majority of instances and that the prospects and rapidity of cure are directly related to the availability and intensity of proper treatment..

All this the correctional system might emulate — and in some progressive jurisdictions it does. Some individuals have to be protected against themselves, some have to be protected from other prisoners, some even from the community. Some mental patients must be detained for a time even against their wishes, and the same is true of offenders. Offenders with propensities for impulsive and predatory aggression should not be permitted to live among us unrestrained by some kind of social control. *But the great majority of offenders, even "criminals," should never become prisoners if we want to "cure" them.*

What we want to accomplish is the reintegration of the temporarily suspended individual back into the main stream of social life, preferably a life at a higher level than before, just as soon as possible. Many, many precariously constituted individuals are trying to make it on the outside right now, with little help from us. We all have to keep reminding ourselves that *most offenders are never even apprehended*. Most of those who are caught and convicted, we must remember,· are released either free or on probation. But they rarely have the benefit of treatment...

Public education and involvement are the first steps in any permanent, constructive change in our wretchedly inadequate, self-destroying, self-injuring, crime-encouraging system...

I have seen it happen. I saw the reaction of the people of Kansas to the discovery of the facts about their wretched state hospitals as exposed by the newspapers in 1948, and I saw the legislators' reactions to the people's reaction...

The people believed what we said, and their legislators voted additional money. The cost *per day* went up five times. But the cost *for each discharged patient* went down *more* than five times. The state mental hospital budget has never since then been an item of political controversy, and not once in nineteen years has it been seriously curtailed.

70

Today there are forty times as many psychiatrists and gradu-ate nurses in the Kansas state hospitals as in 1948. More than forty times as much therapy is given — and there are forty times as many recoveries. And there are forty times forty more private citizens helping with the state mental-health programs as volunteers, companions, foster parents, or staff employees.

PUNISHMENT IS WORTHLESS

We have enough information about the value of punishment to know that it is worthless. It does not foster rehabilitation, nor does it deter. The imposition of pain or humiliation upon an individual will, as any textbook on correction substantiates, isolate and alienate that individual. Punishment fosters attitudes that are incompatible with community living, and may effectively end any hope of modifying the criminal's behavior.

From an untitled essay by Thomas J. Callanan in *Punishment: For And Against*, p. 85, published by Hart Publishing Co. in 1971. Mr. Callanan is a former president of the New York State Probation and Parole Officers Association.

Some day, somewhere, the same thing will happen with respect to transgressors and offenders. It will be harder to bring about, for reasons we have given: the public has a fascination for violence, and clings tenaciously to its yen for vengeance, blind and deaf to the expense, futility, and dangerousness of the resulting penal system. But we are bound to hope that this will yield in time to the persistent, penetrating light of intelligence and accumulating scientific knowledge. The public will grow increasingly ashamed of its cry for retaliation, its persistent demand to punish. This is its crime, *our* crime against criminals — and incidentally our crime against ourselves. For before we can diminish our sufferings from the ill-controlled aggressive assaults of fellow citizens, we must renounce the philosophy of punishment, the obsolete, vengeful penal attitude. In its place we would seek a comprehensive, constructive social attitude — therapeutic in some instances, restraining in some instances, but preventive in its total social impact.

A MATTER OF PERSONAL MORALS

In the last analysis this becomes a question of personal

morals and values. No matter how glorified or how piously disguised, vengeance as a human motive must be personally repudiated by each and every one of us. This is the message of old religions and new psychiatries. Unless this message is heard, unless we, the people — the man on the street, the housewife in the home — can give up our delicious satisfactions in opportunities for vengeful retaliation on scapegoats, we cannot expect to preserve our peace, our public safety, or our mental health.

"It is right, morally right, to be angry with criminals and to express that anger publicly, officially, and in an appropriate manner, which may require the worst of them to be executed."

THE JUSTICE OF PUNISHMENT

Walter Berns

Walter Berns is a Guggenheim Fellow and a resident scholar at the American Enterprise Institute for Public Policy Research in Washington, D.C., on leave from the University of Toronto.

Consider the following questions while reading:

1. **How did the work of Nazi hunter Simon Wiesenthal** *change the author's mind about punishing criminals?*
2. **Why does the author think criminals are the proper** *objects of anger?*
3. **Why does the author think anger against criminals is an** *expression of caring? Do you agree?*

Walter Berns, *For Capital Punishment: Crime and the Morality of the Death Penalty*, published by Basic Books in 1979. Reprinted with permission.

PUNISHING CRIMINALS

Until recently, my business did not require me to think about the punishment of criminals...I was aware of the disagreement among professionals concerning the purpose of punishment — whether it was intended to deter others, to rehabilitate the criminal, or to pay him back — but like most laymen I had no particular reason to decide which purpose was right or to what extent they may all have been right. I did know that retribution was held in ill repute among criminologists and jurists — to them, retribution was a fancy name for revenge, and revenge was barbaric...

THE EXAMPLE OF SIMON WIESENTHAL

It was the phenomenon of Simon Wiesenthal that allowed me to understand why the intellectuals were wrong and why the police, the politicians, and the majority of the voters were right: we punish criminals principally in order to pay them back, and we execute the worst of them out of moral necessity. Anyone who respects Wiesenthal's mission will be driven to the same conclusion.

PUNISHMENT MAINTAINS SOCIAL ORDER

Were the law to be deprived of the instruments of punishment, it would become the essence of futility, and the social order would collapse. Punishment makes possible the dignity and the integrity of law. To imagine that we could ever abolish punishment would be to entertain the fantasy that we could endure without law. The issue of punishment is, in a word, the issue of law

From an untitled essay by Roy Eckardt in *Punishment: For And Against*, published by Hart Publishing Co., in 1971, p. 172. Dr. Eckardt is Professor of Religion at Lehigh University and the author of numerous books on religion.

Of course, not everyone will respect that mission. It will strike the busy man—I mean the sort of man who sees things only in the light cast by a concern for his own interests—as somewhat bizarre. Why should anyone devote his life—more than thirty years of it!—exclusively to the task of hunting down the Nazi war criminals who survived World War II and escaped punishment? Wiesenthal says his conscience forces him "to bring the guilty ones to trial." But why punish them? What do we hope to accomplish now by punishing SS Obersturmbannfuhrer Franz Stangl or someday—who knows?—Reichsleiter Martin Bormann? We surely don't expect to rehabilitate them, and it would be foolish to think that by punishing them we might thereby deter others. The answer, I think, is clear: We want to punish them in order *to pay them back*. We think they must be made to pay for their crimes with their lives, and we think that we, the survivors of the world they violated, may legitimately exact that payment because we, too, are their victims. By punishing them, we demonstrate that there are laws that bind men across generations as well as across (and within) nations, that we are not simply isolated individuals, each pursuing his selfish interests and connected with others by a mere contract to live and let live. To state it simply, Wiesenthal allows us to see that it is right, morally right, to be angry with criminals and to express that anger publicly, officially, and in an appropriate manner, which may require the worst of them to be executed.

PUNISHMENT ADVANCES HUMAN DIGNITY

Modern civil-libertarian opponents of capital punishment do not understand this. They say that to execute a criminal is to deny his human dignity...they are essentially selfish men, distrustful of passion, who do not understand the connection between anger and justice, and between anger and human dignity.

Anger is expressed or manifested on those occasions when someone has acted in a manner that is thought to be unjust, and one of its origins is the opinion that men are responsible, and should be held responsible, for what they do...Anger, then, is a very human passion not only because only a human being can be angry, but also because anger acknowledges the humanity of its objects: it holds them accountable for what they do. And in holding particular men responsible, it pays them the respect that is due them as men. Anger recognizes that only men have the capacity to be moral beings and, in so doing, acknowledges the dignity of human beings. Anger is somehow connected with justice, and it is this that modern penology has not understood; it tends, on the whole, to regard anger as a selfish indulgence.

Anger can, of course, be that; and if someone does not become angry with an insult or an injury suffered unjustly, we tend to think he does not think much of himself...

CONCERN FOR OTHERS REQUIRES PUNISHMENT

If men are not saddened when someone else suffers, or angry when someone else suffers unjustly, the implication is that they do not care for anyone other than themselves or that they lack some quality that befits a man. When we criticize them for this, we acknowledge that they ought to care for others. If men are not angry when a neighbor suffers at the hands of a criminal, the implication is that their moral faculties have been corrupted, that they are not good citizens.

THE GREATEST EVIL

SOCRATES: *Is not our conclusion then that injustice and the doing of wrong is the greatest of evils?*
POLUS: *Evidently.*
SOCRATES: *And it was shown that punishment rids us of this evil?*
POLUS: *Apparently.*
SOCRATES: *And when punishment is evaded, the evil abides?*
POLUS: *Yes.*
SOCRATES: *Then wrongdoing itself holds the second place among evils, but first and greatest of all evils is to do wrong and escape punishment.*
POLUS: *So it seems.*

From *The Collected Dialogues of Plato*, Edited by E. Hamilton & H. Cairns, p. 263.

Criminals are properly the objects of anger, and the perpetrators of terrible crimes—for example, Lee Harvey Oswald and James Earl Ray—are properly the objects of great anger. They have done more than inflict an injury on an isolated individual; they have violated the foundations of trust and friendship, the necessary elements of a moral community, the only community worth living in. A moral community, unlike a hive of bees or a hill of ants, is one whose members are expected freely to obey the laws and, unlike those in tyranny, are trusted to obey the laws. The criminal has violated that trust, and in so doing has injured not merely his immediate victim but the community as such. He has called into question the very possibility of that community by suggesting that men cannot be trusted to respect freely the property, the person, and the dignity of those with whom they are associated. If, then, men are not angry when someone else is robbed, raped, or murdered, the implication is that no moral community exists, because those men do not care for anyone other than themselves. Anger is an expression of that caring, and society needs men who care for one another, who share their pleasures and their pains, and do so for the sake of the others.

> *"Ideally, sentences imposed by judges should be divided into three parts (punishment, isolation and rehabilitation), each to be served sequentially and in an appropriate place designed to fulfill only that one purpose well."*

THREE KINDS OF PRISONS NEEDED

Alan F. Kay

Alan F. Key is president of Halcyon House, an organization for the promotion of social justice, based in Weston, Massachusetts.

Consider the following questions while reading:
1. **What are the three purposes of prisons, according to the author?**
2. **Why are punishment and rehabilitation at cross-purposes, according to the author?**
3. **Why does the author think three different kinds of prisons are needed? Do you agree?**

THREE PURPOSES FOR PRISON

Three distinct purposes constitute the fundamental justification for the existence of prisons and serve to define the prison system in America. These are: 1) punishment, whether for retribution, expiation or deterrence; 2) incapacitation, also called long-term isolation, protection of society by keeping criminals locked away; and 3) rehabilitation.

The Supreme Court, with broad public support, has taken the position that a prison should serve all three purposes...

Could a society exist without punishment? Is there any possibility that America will give up punishment in the next 50 years? Those tempted to answer yes to either question should consider the value of general deterrence in keeping down white-collar crime...common sense tells us that even the possibility of going to jail, which is so repugnant to most middle-class people, plays a significant role in the prevention of a potentially enormous amount of white-collar crime.

Incapacitation or long-term isolation is often considered by humanitarians as the most ineffective and repugnant purpose of prisons and yet it is a tautology that convicted criminals, as long as they are locked away from society, cannot commit new crimes against society outside. There have, in fact, been studies that have concluded that isolation is the only method that can be shown statistically to reduce crime rates...

CROSS-PURPOSES

If we examine the three purposes of prisons closely, we find that to a surprising degree they are at cross-purposes to each other. One cannot punish someone and expect to rehabilitate him at the same time. Rehabilitation, to be effective, must be presented as a good and desirable activity for the recipient. Punishment must be perceived by him as undesirable or it is not punishment. Rehabilitation, if it means anything, means helping a person make his or her way back into society, and isolation means keeping a person locked away from society. A certain amount of education or training may be imparted during isolation that may eventually help with rehabilitation, but that is as far as one can go in linking these two purposes.

The conflict between punishment and isolation is more subtle but equally severe. Since isolation is deprivation of liberty, long-term isolation is, even theoretically, very punishing. In real prison systems it is often so brutal and offensive as to be more inhumane than those cruel and unusual violations of human rights: flogging, stocks and even capital punishment...

THREE PRISONS NEEDED

The three methods — punishment, isolation and rehabilitation — should be separated both in place and time to the maximum extent possible. Ideally, sentences imposed by judges should be divided into three parts (punishment, isolation and rehabilitation), each to be served sequentially and in an appropriate place designed to fulfill only that one purpose well. Let us call these places: punishment prisons, isolation prisons and rehabilitation facilities. Within each of the three categories several different kinds of prisons, camps, settings or facilities are desirable. These can be obtained by reorienting existing facilities, in general without great expense. Nothing in this proposal should be construed as requiring three consecutive sentences for every conviction. It is assumed that in most cases only one or two of the facilities will be used.

REHABILITATION OR DETTERENCE?

An institution built to carry out society's moral precepts through punishment and deterrence cannot also function as an effective means to rehabilitate the offender. An institution so secure that it will tolerate no escape and no threat of riot, for example, is unlikely to offer a relaxed and therapeutic atmosphere conducive to self-reflection and positive efforts at self-change. The very characteristics that are essential to punishment are insuperable obstacles to rehabilitation.

From Norval Morris and James Jacobs, *Proposals for Prison Reform*, published by the Public Affairs Committee, Inc., July 1974.

PUNISHMENT

For example, in white-collar crime, probably only punishment is required. Certainly John Mitchell and other Watergate criminals did not need to be isolated to protect society, nor did they require rehabilitation. The rest of us might envy their ability to make their way back financially with sales of rights to biographies and novels alone. What they did require was punishment, which they did not get, except, of course, for a temporary and benign deprivation of liberty...

Probably only chronic offenders or psychotic criminals should require an isolation facility. For others, often only a short-term punishment (less than one week) or a minor punishment plus some rehabilitation will be appropriate. A small "dose" of punishment may be all that is necessary for most first offenders.

Each part of a sentence should conform to appropriate statutory requirements and be thoughtfully imposed to accomplish all of society's needs. Case by case, a composite sentence must be imposed suitable to the crime and to the criminal, taking into consideration the availability under the plan of separate facilities optimized for each purpose...

Although there will be some overlapping of methods in the three kinds of facilities, the key point is that the priority purpose must always be clear. In those instances where it may be possible to achieve some rehabilitation during isolation or where isolation is in fact punishment, the purpose which takes priority will always be clear.

ISOLATION

When under this proposal the punishment phase of each sentence is ended, society will in effect be saying to the world at large that this prisoner has been punished enough. Therefore, the isolation prison which the sentence may call for in the next phase must have no aspect of punishment beyond a) the minimum implicit in forced isolation from society and b) whatever is necessary for good order...

Thus in the design, equipping and location of isolation prisons, all vindictiveness must be removed.

REHABILITATION

The third purpose, rehabilitation, is unique because it alone seeks the prisoner's cooperation. Since the need for and the possibilities for rehabilitation in a given instance cannot be adequately judged until the time for rehabilitation is at hand, a review procedure by a rehabilitation board is required (except for sentences that impose neither punishment nor isolation prison, when the function can be handled by the original sentencing judge). The rehabilitation board is somewhat similar to present parole boards but has an authorization quite different. The time of first consideration of each case by the rehabilitation board is set by the original sentencing judge (as part of the sentence) and must be sometime prior to the end of the isolation prison term. The board at that time must make a determination whether the prisoner should start his rehabilitation in an isolation prison which has some rehabilitation facilities or only after the isolation sentence has been completed.

HUMANITARIAN REFORM

Most people who speak of prison reform do not differentiate between two distinct concepts: humanitarian reform *and* the rehabilitative ideal. *Humanitarian reform calls for minimum civilized standards of living conditions and of physical safety within the prison. The rehabilitative ideal refers to the kind of treatment that will bring about the successful reintegration of prisoners into society.*

It is possible to speak of humanitarian prison reform without even mentioning the word rehabilitation. Since our institutions — schools, hospitals, nursing homes as well as prisons — reflect the character of our society and the kind of people we are, we owe it to ourselves to maintain them in a way that will not shame us.

From Norval Morris and James Jacobs, *Proposals for Prison Reform*, published by the Public Affairs Committee, Inc., July 1974.

When the isolation sentence is completed in either case, the board must review the case and determine if the prisoner is to be assigned to a halfway house or other rehabilitation facility or released to freedom with some rehabilitation benefits, such as an opportunity to live in a subsidized community or apartment for a period of time or to have subsidized vocational training or other education. These options are the prerogative of the board. Should the prisoner fail to cooperate or take advantage of the rehabilitation program, the rehabilitation board may review its position and reassign the prisoner within its prerogatives. In no case, however, can the board confine the prisoner for longer than his original sentence. This faces up to the fact that some criminals cannot be rehabilitated, although every effort should be made to keep the proportion as low as possible. No authority for punishment or isolation is given the rehabilitation board beyond that necessary for its rehabilitation purpose. The only sentences for punishment and isolation are to be meted out by the judge at the time of original conviction.

CONCLUSIONS

There are a number of reasons why the proposed prison system can achieve crime rate reductions that cannot be achieved in a prison system where all three purposes are pursued essentially at the same time or in the same facility with the same administration and guards.

First, at any time in the course of imprisonment, the convict himself, the guards and the prison administration (and, should they ever become involved, political officials, judges and the general public) all know precisely what purpose is being served by the imprisonment. All actions, programs and results can be judged by their contribution to the effectiveness of the single and nonconflicting priority purpose...

The second reason is that guards and administration may be organized, selected and trained in a manner suitable for the single function of each facility...

The final and most intriguing reason for expecting improvement in the new system is grounded in hard practical psychology which everyone can understand. Human beings, whether saints or sinners, often with amazing tenacity resist being won over to any program, way of life or philosophy whose protagonists are simultaneously inflicting physical, mental or spiritual punishment on them. This is true whether such punishment is deserved or not or whether it comes by judicial blessing or by the efforts of guards to control prisoners by intimidation, harassment, isolation or other means. Punishment is certainly unlikely to be totally eliminated for many years, if ever. However, when punishment is over for a given prisoner as it is during the isolation and rehabilitation phases, society has its best chance of beginning to win over that prisoner. Similarly, isolation prisons without vindictiveness give society its best chance of making the prisoner more amenable to a successful rehabilitation phase. And rehabilitation is most successful when it can be conducted outside of a prison setting, without punishment, isolation or compulsion.

RANKING PRISON PURPOSES

Instructions

STEP 1
Working in groups of four to six students, each group should rank the prison purposes listed, in the order the group thinks is the most important. Assign the number 1 to the purpose the group believes is most important. Assign the number 2 to the second most important purpose, and so on, until all the purposes have been ranked.

STEP 2
Each group should compare its ranking with others in the class in a classwide discussion.

PURPOSES OF PRISON

_____ a. *Deterrence* of the potential criminal is one purpose of prisons. If A is punished, B will be frightened of the consequences and refrain from committing a crime.

_____ b. Prisons exist to *protect society by isolating* those who commit anti-social acts such as murder, rape, assault, and theft.

_____ c. *Repayment of a debt* to society is another purpose of prisons. It is based on an age-old belief that justice is, in effect, measurable.

_____ d. *Punishment* is the most ancient purpose for prisons. Deprivation of freedom is the appropriate punishment for those who have violated the social compact with society.

_____ e. The purpose of prisons is to *provide custody and treatment* based on the individual needs of the offenders with the purpose of rehabilitating them and redeeming them from their criminal ways.

_____ f. Another purpose served by prisons is that of helping *avoid facing certain unpleasant realities* by warehousing criminals away from public view.

_____ e. Rank any *other purposes* you think should be included.

Chapter **3**

AMERICA'S PRISONS

Can Prisons Rehabilitate?

"It would be an exaggeration to say that no treatment methods work...but certainly, few programs seem to succeed."

THE FAILURE OF REHABILITATION

The Committee for the Study of Incarceration

The Committee for the Study of Incarceration was created and funded by the Field Foundation, the New World Foundation and the Lawyer's Committee for Civil Rights Under Law. Over a dozen scholars and experts from various fields were committee members. The principal author of the committee's report, from which this viewpoint was taken, is Andrew Von Hirsch, Associate Professor of Criminal Justice at Rutgers University. The report was published in 1976.

Consider the following questions while reading:
1. **How does the committee distinguish rehabilitation from punishment?**
2. **Why does the Committee claim the rehabilitative model has not worked? What examples does it present?**

From *Doing Justice: The Choice of Punishments* by Andrew Von Hirsch. Copyright © 1976 by Andrew Von Hirsch. Reprinted by permission of Hill and Wang, a division of Farrar, Straus & Giroux, Inc.

WHAT IS REHABILITATION?

Rehabilitation. During the last century and a half, this concept has dominated penal philosophy and rhetoric. It is part of a humanistic tradition which, in pressing for ever more individualization of justice, has demanded that we treat the criminal, not the crime. It relies upon a medical and educative model, defining the criminal as, if not sick, less than evil; somehow less "responsible" than he had previously been regarded. As a kind of social malfunctioner, the criminal needs to be "treated" or to be reeducated, reformed, or rehabilitated. Rehabilitation is, in many ways, the opposite of punishment...

THE REHABILITATIVE MODEL HAS NOT WORKED

Part of the inherent definition of a sick person is a presumption of non-culpability for his disease; when we say "It's not his fault, he is sick," we are defining the patient as the victim, not the victimizer. This was an especially attractive premise for the humane and optimistic legal philosophers.

But the therapeutic model is a complicated one. To some members of the Committee, it still may hold the highest ideal, and they abandon it with great reluctance. Crucial practical and moral difficulties are encountered, however, when this ideal is incorporated into the compulsory processes of the criminal law. The simple fact is that the experiment has not worked out. Despite every effort and every attempt, correctional treatment programs have failed. The supporters of rehabilitation will say, and perhaps rightly so, that it was never really given a complete chance that it was only accepted in theory while in practice the system has insisted on maintaining punitive practices. On the other hand, the question remains whether one can reasonably continue to expect anything different, given the extended trial that rehabilitation has had.

Moreover, the rehabilitative model, despite its emphasis on understanding and concern, has been more cruel and punitive than a frankly punitive model would probably be. Medicine is allowed to be bitter; inflicted pain is not cruelty, if it is treatment rather than punishment. Under the rehabilitative model, we have been able to abuse our charges, the prisoners, without disabusing our consciences. Beneath this cloak of benevolence, hypocrisy has flourished, and each new exploitation of the prisoner has inevitably been introduced as an act of grace. Finally, to sentence people guilty of similar crimes to different dispositions in the name of rehabilitation — to punish not for act but for condition — violates, this book argues, fundamental concepts of equity and fairness. And so we as a group, trained in humanistic traditions, have ironically embraced the seemingly harsh principle of just deserts...

Proponents of correctional treatment once had reason to complain that their methods had never really been given a chance to work. Prison administrators, while long on talk about rehabilitation, were short on programs: the available "treatments" did little more than train convicts in skills for which there existed no market in the outside world, such as making license plates. But during recent decades — especially in California — seriously thought-out and well-financed experimental programs have been tried. The results have not been encouraging.

THE PROFESSIONAL CRIMINAL

The professional criminal who looks upon crime of a certain sort — preferably highly organized — as a means of achieving a very prosperous way of life. He chuckles at the old saw that crime does not pay, since he knows at first hand that it pays very well.

Again, there is nothing the penologist can do to change the attitudes of such criminals once convicted. The only lesson they learn is that they must be more careful next time. Once released, they will, of course, return to the old activity. It is important to understand that such criminals are not neurotic because they deviate from the social norm. They simply have a different ethic than the ordinary man. "Let the majority of people play it straight, and I will take advantage of their stupidity by cutting corners."

The professional criminal with this ethic is entirely beyond the pale of the analyst or psychiatrist. He is incapable of feeling a sense of guilt — either neurotic or genuine.

From an untitled essay by Edward Madden in *Punishment: For and Against*, pp. 137-38.

Ask a warden or prison psychologist why his favorite rehabilitation program is effective, and he may tell you he has seen it work: former incorrigibles who participated now keep out of trouble. But that "proof" is illusory: for the "cured" individuals might have stopped offending without any program — because of advancing age, diminishing criminal opportunities, or whatever...

I HAVE MURDERED
21 HUMAN BEINGS

I have no desire whatever to reform myself. My only desire is to reform people who try to reform me. And I believe that the only way to reform people is to kill 'em...

In my lifetime I have murdered 21 human beings, I have committed thousands of burglaries, robberies, larcenies, arsons and last but not least I have committed sodomy on more than 1,000 male human beings. For all of these things I am not the least bit sorry. I have no conscience so that does not worry me. I don't believe in man, God nor Devil. I hate the whole damned human race including myself.

From Carl Panzram #31614, *Killer; A Journal of Murder* by Thomas E. Gaddis and James O. Long, MacMillan Company, 1970.

DISAPPOINTING RESULTS

A wide variety of rehabilitation programs have now been studied. A few successes have been reported, but the overall results are disappointing...Thus, for example:

• The character of the institution seems to have little or no influence on recidivism. It was hoped that prisoners in smaller and less regimented institutions would return to crime less often on release, but that hope has not been borne out.[1]

• Although probation has long been acclaimed for its rehabilitative usefulness, the recidivism rate among otherwise like offenders fails to show a clear difference whether they are placed on probation or confined. While those on probation perform no worse, the claim that they perform better has not been sustained.[2]

• More intensive supervision on the streets, a recurring theme in rehabilitation, has not been shown to curb recidivism. Probationers or parolees assigned to small caseloads with intense supervision appear to return to crime about as often as those assigned to large caseloads with minimal supervision.[3]

• Vocational training has been widely advocated, on the theory that people turn to crime because they lack the skills enabling them to earn a lawful living. The quality of many programs has been poor. But where well-staffed and well-equipped programs of vocational training for marketable skills have been tried in institutions, studies fail to show a lower rate of return to crime.[4] In California, where this technique has most extensively been used, authorities have all but given up hope...

• In the late 1960s, "community-based" treatment received increased emphasis. It was thought that offenders' chances for being rehabilitated would be enhanced if the treatment were undertaken in their home neighborhoods. Some of these "community-based" programs consisted of intensive counseling or other therapy conducted in small, residential facilities located in low-income neighborhoods; others consisted of daytime treatment programs that allowed the participants to live at home. Results thus far have not been encouraging[5]...

It would be an exaggeration to say that no treatment methods work, for some positive results have been reported, which further follow-up may confirm. But, certainly, few programs seem to succeed.

1. Support for predictive restraint alone, without rehabilitation, is found in the 1973 report of the National Advisory Commission on Criminal Justice Stand Goals, NACCJSG, *Corrections*, Commentary on Standard 5.3: "...there are some offenders whose aggressive, repetitive, violent, or predatory behavior poses a serious threat to the community. In many instances, these offenders are not responsive to correctional programs. Public safety may require that they be incapacitated for a period of time in excess of 5 years."
A 1974 statement by William Saxbe, then the United States Attorney General, also exemplifies this philosophy. In a reported speech to the International Association of Chiefs of Police, he said: " 'Too many dangerous convicted offenders are placed back in society in one way or another, and that simply must stop.'...Mr. Saxbe departed from his prepared text to deliver a free-wheeling attack on 'starry-eyed' theorists whose view of prison as an instrument of rehabilitation...results in the return to society of dangerous, hardened criminals with no intention of going straight...'Prosecutors, court and parole boards must face the fact that some violent offenders cannot be rehabilitated,' he declared. 'Dangerous and violent offenders...should know that arrest means conviction and conviction means prison.' " "Saxbe and Kelley, Citing Crime Rise, Hold Prosecutors and Courts Guilty," *New York Times*, Sept. 24, 1974, p. 18.
2. *Model Sentencing Act*, preface.
3. Alan M. Dershowitz, "The Law of Dangerousness: Some Fictions about Predictions," 23 *J. Legal Ed.* 24, 26 (1970).
4. E. W. Burgess, "Factors Determining Success or Failure on Parole," in *The Working of The Indeterminate Sentence Law of Illinois*, ed. by A. A. Bruce, A. G. Haino, and E. W. Burgess (Springfield, Ill.: State Board of Parole, 1928).
5. For citation in footnote: Harry L. Kozol, Richard J. Boucher, and Ralph F. Garofalo, "The Diagnosis and Treatment of Dangerousness," 18 *Crime and Delinquency* 371 (1972).

ALTERNATIVE 2

"Rehabilitation is often a miracle worker. Sometimes, it has consisted in teaching illiterates to read and write. Sometimes, it has been the teaching of a useful trade...but has rehabilitation ever 'cured' anyone or reformed his criminal tendencies? The answer to that is yes."

REHABILITATION WORKS

Karl Menninger

Karl Menninger, M.S. is a distinguished psychiatrist and author. For many years he has been an advocate of prison reform. His most recent book is *Whatever Became of Sin?*

Consider the following questions while reading:
1. **Why does Dr. Menninger favor rehabilitation programs?**
2. **What does Dr. Menninger mean when he says rehabilitation is not a cure or a treatment?**
3. **Do you think his ideas on rehabilitation are realistic?**

Karl Menninger, "Doing True Justice," *America*, July 9, 1977, pp. 6-9. Reprinted with permission of America Press, Inc., 106 West 56th Street, New York, N.Y. 10019 © 1977 All rights reserved.

The Committee for the Study of Incarceration, created and funded by the Field Foundation, the New World Foundation and the Lawyers' Committee for Civil Rights Under Law, has added to the interminable dialogue with its long-awaited report presented in the form of a book entitled: *Doing Justice: The Choice of Punishments, Report of the Committee for the Study of Incarceration...*

REHABILITATION PROGRAMS THAT WORK

There are silly words in this book about the failure and demise of the "rehabilitation model." Rehabilitation, as Dr. Gaylin and I know it professionally in our psychiatric hospitals and in some of the better prisons, is a vigorous, worthy, helpful program. It includes much body-restoring technology, flavored sometimes with the over-optimism of wistful hope. Marvelous institutions, such as Dr. Rusk's Institute at New York University, are famous for their work with amputees and paraplegics and otherwise crippled people. The same work goes on in scores of Veterans' Administration hospitals with patients whose physical and mental plights distress us all and whose benefits, under rehabilitation, are often miraculous. For mentally ill sufferers, as well as for blind, deaf and crippled people, wonderful coping devices, teaching methods and fields of activities have been developed in millieu therapy. This was furthered throughout the nation by the late, indefatigable humanitarian and public servant, Mary Switzer, in the Rehabilitation Department of Health, Education and Welfare. It was welcomed and applauded and advocated by my brother Will Menninger and myself in Topeka. It was installed in Army, Navy and Veterans' Administration hospitals, in state and private psychiatric hospitals *and in many prisons.*

I have helped to develop these rehabilitation methods and programs and to extend them into correctional programs. I therefore resent the mournful references in this book to their failure in prisons, as if it was the rehabilitation and not the prison milieu that was intrinsically weak or ineffective. Admittedly, even for prisoners and even in prisons, rehabilitation is often a miracle worker. Sometimes, it has consisted in teaching illiterates to read and write. Sometimes, it has been the teaching of a useful trade. Sometimes, it has been an introduction to music and art for a human being who scarcely knew they existed.

But has rehabilitation ever "cured" anyone or reformed his criminal tendencies? The answer to that is yes. It may not have prevented recidivism in some poor Chicano who, alas, lived to starve and steal again. It may not have succeeded in restraining some black lad of moronic intelligence level from joining old chums in another escapade. Nor did it perhaps prevent some hapless "reformed" ex-convict from forging another check on a hard, dark day. This is the sort of evidence often used to show that rehabilitation efforts are a failure. Many other questions could just as well be asked, questions with sad answers. But does rehabilitation give thousands of idle men something to do while enjoying the miseries of our techniques of incarceration? Does it teach some of them a trade or craft? Does it make prison life more bearable or less dehumanizing? I think it does.

REHABILITATION IS SELFISH

There is no age, type of crime, amount of sentence, or length of incarceration, that makes a person rehabilitatible. He or She must reach a stage in their lives where they are tired of what they are like, where they have been and the direction they are heading. Rehabilitation is a selfish state of mind, a person rehabilitates for their own personal purpose. No one can force this state upon himself, nor can any group or organization. Programs can only be placed at the convenience of the person, so he can utilize it when he unconsciously decides to change. If too many obstacles are placed in his path, restrictions by the administraton, then that person could very well pass the stage that would be most productive for him and take a downward trend.

From "Rehabilitation," *The Angolite*, March/April 1979, by inmate number 79666.

REHABILITATION IS NOT A CURE

The introduction to this book says that rehabilitation is on the decline because "it abandoned with internal inconsistencies...opportunities for exploitation...unexpected abhorrent consequences..." and proved "less humane or liberal than its proponents had anticipated" (p. xxxvii).

Some of that may be true. Rehabilitation is not a cure; it really is not a treatment. It is an attitude concerned with developing capabilities and not with the "deserts" that this committee considers so solemnly. One fine rehabilitation program we ran in the Illinois prisons included instruction and training in truck driving. We trained some excellent drivers from abundant eager material. The prisoners loved it. The officials were proud of it. But the graduates, when released, almost immediately learned that none of them could use their skills. They could not legally obtain a driver's license for five years! Five years is a long time between meals, and children get hungry. Some parolees could not wait that long. (Governor Ogilvie helped us to resolve this particular roadblock and dozens of others through the skillful and effective administration of Commissioner Peter Bensinger, now in Washington.)...

I believe that some fellow citizens transgress the laws and that two or three percent of these, particularly the poor, dull, black and friendless ones, are collected by the police and ultimately lodged in prison. I well know that a number of these are mean, ugly, vicious and dangerous persons. My wife and I have been the victims of some of them. They should not be released on the excuse that they are "insane" or pitiable or rich or young. They should not be released at all, until they have undergone some demonstrable change for the better and are no longer violent people. I would also put some of the seldom confined offenders among these, the child beaters, wife abusers and vandals.

I also know that some of these men are not beyond at least partial redemption, i.e., change in life style toward socialization, even in the rotten milieu we put them into in the name of punishment. Many of them will learn to be better criminals, and I do not refer here to moral improvement. I do not want dangerous men around me or near my family or near anyone else. I want the state to protect us from their divinations and conspiracies and impulses to rob and hurt. But I want the state to restrain them with effectiveness, decency, kindness and sureness.

Rehabilitation simply means trying to help some handicapped people, who can accept it, to help themselves, like a child being taught to ride a bicycle. I cannot concede that rehabilitation is a weak modality or a despised objective. It may not prevent them, after release from our persecution of them, from ever committing another crime. Faced with new opportunities for shooting craps, stealing tires, forging checks or shoplifting, they may again yield to their impulses of greed or vengeance...

My comments will no doubt give rise to renewed accusations that I am a "mollycoddler" and a "bleeding heart." If by mollycoddling is meant having sympathy for sufferers, whether victims of themselves or of others, whether physical or social or mental sufferers, I may well be guilty. But I am no ascetic saint, dedicated to trying to like unpleasant people. I do recognize them as people, not wild animals. As suffering human beings, they have my sympathy.

"We have yet to find one study that reports basic and lasting change in criminal subjects."

THE CRIMINAL PERSONALITY

Samuel Yochelson & Stanton E. Samenow

The following viewpoint is taken from *The Criminal Personality*, volume two, which reports the results of 16 years of work with criminal patients at St. Elizabeth's Hospital in Washington, D.C. Yochelson and Samenow studied the personalities of 240 men, spending hundreds of hours with many of them and as many as 8,000 hours with a few. Dr. Yochelson was a respected neuropsychiatrist who died in 1976. Dr. Samenow, who teaches psychiatry at George Washington University School of Medicine, published the second volume of the study in 1977, from which this viewpoint is taken.

Consider the following questions while you read:
1. How do the authors define the word criminal?
2. How do they describe the criminal profile?
3. What image does the criminal have of himself?
4. What observations do they make about rehabilitating criminals?

The dimensions of the task of changing a criminal[1] to a responsible person are poorly understood. The procedures that have been used with criminals have not been effective. Crime is still very much with us and, indeed, according to statistics, is a more formidable problem today than ever before. Previous efforts at rehabilitation have failed for two main reasons: there has been insufficient knowledge of what the criminal is — his thinking processes and behavior patterns — and the techniques used have almost all been adaptations of techniques used with noncriminals...

THE CRIMINAL PROFILE

At an early age, the criminal-to-be makes a series of choices that involve going counter to the responsible forces that prevail in all socioeconomic levels. Even in the high-crime areas, most of his contemporaries do not choose a criminal path. However, as a youngster, the criminal finds the restraints of responsible living unacceptable and even contemptible. He rejects the requirements and way of life of parents, siblings, teachers, employers, and others in his environment who are responsible.

Although he may manage to convince others that he is responsible and, through a facade of conformity, keep society at bay while pursuing his criminal objectives, he scorns such social institutions as the school, the church, and the law.

To be like the responsible children in his neighborhood and at school is to be a "nothing." The criminal child wants something different. He usually begins his violating patterns at home. Then if he cannot find the excitement that he wants in his own surroundings, he goes where he can find it. Crime does not come to the criminal-to-be; he goes to it...

---

1. Readers familiar with volume 1 of this work know that rather than limit our definition of a criminal to a person convicted of a crime, we have presented a more comprehensive profile of the criminal as a person whose *patterns of thinking* have led to arrestable behavior. These we have called "criminal thinking patterns." While some of the "criminal thinking patterns" may be found in the noncriminal, they lead not to arrestability but rather to ineffectiveness. All of the irresponsible thinking patterns in the criminal described in volume 1 must be altered in the change process presented in this volume. It is essential to underscore that the person with whom we are working is indeed a criminal, even though, regardless of the number or seriousness of the crimes he has committed, he regards himself as a good person. The reader is referred to volume 1 for a detailed description of criminal patterns of thinking and action.

The criminal disregards other people's right to live safely, but demands that others show him the utmost respect and consideration. He breaks promises; in fact, he never regards a promise as a promise unless it is part of a larger operation to secure something for himself. It does not bother him to injure others; he rarely sees anything from another's point of view. Although society considers him harmful, the criminal believes that he is exercising a right to live as he chooses...

The criminal has such a different frame of reference that even simple words like friend, love, *and* trust *have meanings radically different from conventional usage.*

The criminal lives in a world where there is no loyalty or trust, even in relation to others like him. Untrustworthy himself, he demands that others trust him. If he happens to earn others' trust, he exploits it. He depends on others but does not see his own dependence. To him, this exhibits weakness and places him in jeopardy. He claims he can live without interdependence but demands that others provide him with whatever he wants. The criminal does not know how to get along with responsible people from day to day; he generally occupies the extremes of total withdrawal or inappropriate intimacy. He is tolerant of others' shortcomings but reacts angrily when anyone finds fault with him. Instead of friendships, the criminal seeks avenues of triumph. People are to be used, conquered, controlled like pawns, exploited...

THE CRIMINAL'S SELF IMAGE

One of the most striking features of the criminal is his view of himself as a good person. Despite all the injuries he has inflicted on others, he does not consider himself a criminal. His idea of "right" is subjective in the extreme: whatever he wants to do at a given moment is right. If at that time he considered an act wrong for him and regarded himself as an evil person, he would not act as he does. What society calls crime, the criminal regards as his work. When he is required to defend himself, he strives to convince others that they are wrong and that he is right. The criminal's view of himself as a good person constitutes an enormous obstacle to those who seek to rehabilitate him, and an examiner or agent of change encounters a formidable array of tactics that are designed in part to support his view but are actually further expressions of criminal thinking patterns...

REHABILITATING CRIMINALS

Organic treatments (psychosurgery, medication, etc.) have been unsuccessful. The numerous programs for altering an environment that is thought to produce crime have resulted in the expenditure of manpower, money, and energy but have left crime a domestic problem of top priority. Criminals have taken advantage of these programs and demanded more benefits and services, typically selecting what they want and contributing nothing productive to society. Criminals have been given more and more opportunities to change instead of long terms in confinement. Because of a trend toward community-based corrections, criminals have participated in community education and vocational training programs and have lived in community facilities, such as halfway houses, rather than in prisons. These opportunities have not resulted in change from criminal to responsible citizen. Job skills and education that criminals have acquired either have been utilized in the promotion of further crime or have been abandoned altogether. With the return of criminals to the community, the number of crimes committed is extremely high. Criminals have exploited psychotherapeutic work, especially efforts to reconstruct their past to find out why they are the way they are. If a criminal did not have enough excuses for crime before psychotherapy, he has many more after it...

With respect to behavior modification, we find it to be a simplistic way of dealing with a complex problem. Learning particular skills and changing isolated behavioral patterns do not produce basic change in criminals. Using conditioning

---

Only rarely does the criminal genuinely "like" another person. His liking is based on someone's agreeing with him, building him up, assisting him in his plans, or at least not interfering with him. He also "likes" someone he can exploit. His very characteristics preclude his genuinely loving anyone. He regards kindness as weakness. Although he expresses fragments of sentimentality, the criminal cold-bloodedly uses the very people he professes to love.

---

with criminals is like trying to stave off a tidal wave with a bucket. No system of reward and punishment by itself can penetrate and change the thinking processes described in volume 1. Teaching a criminal how to interact agreeably with his teachers or employers and training him with vocational knowhow do not reach the inner man. Manipulating external contingencies and giving rewards do not touch the core of the problem. The criminal is still a criminal. He learns new skills or habits easily enough but uses them to further criminal objectives. He satisfies society's requirements in a token manner, but the payoffs that society offers do not satisfy him. A criminal child may value the greater freedom that he earns when he cooperates at home and at school. But he uses that freedom to advance objectives that cause harm to others. We have yet to find one study that reports basic and lasting change in criminal subjects. Although impressive results have been achieved with behavior modification in noncriminals, this has not been the case with criminals.

SURVIVAL?

I know how to steal. I know how to be hard on broads. I know how to stick somebody up better than anything. I know how to take a small amount of narcotics and eventually work it way up and make me some money. Fencing property or credit cards, I know how to do all that. But society says all that's wrong. I feel like it's survival, making the dollar. I don't have nothing against a guy that makes a dollar. Whatever his bag is, that's his bag.

From *Assualt With A Deadly Weapon: The Autobiography of a Street Criminal* by John Allen, edited by Dianne Kelly and Philip Heymann, published in 1977 by Pantheon Books.

"Until there is a place in our social system for the human products of our prisons, ex-convicts will continue to support themselves through violence."

LET'S GIVE REHABILITATION A CHANCE

Robert Joe Stout

Robert Stout is a free-lance writer who lives in Chico, California.

Consider the following questions while reading:
1. **What practical problems do released prisoners encounter?**
2. **Why does the author think prison rehabilitation and job training programs are unsatisfactory?**
3. **What suggestions for improving prison rehabilitation does the author make?**

Robert Joe Stout, "Why Rahabilitation Hasn't Worked," Copyright 1979 Christian Century Foundation. Reprinted by permission from the July 18-25, 1979 issue of *The Christian Century*, pp. 734-36.

THE EX-CON'S PROBLEM

At 24 a tanned, outdoorsy young man with flashing blue eyes and a sharp tongue, Jimmy was gregarious, personable and willing to do any man a favor. On meeting him, one might deduce that he was the type to get into a fight at a western dance — he was only 5'4" and exhibited the feisty belligerence of a person who compensates for his size by becoming overly aggressive — but no one would label him a "criminal type" unless it were known that he'd spent seven of the past 11 years in adult and juvenile lockups...

Like many other recidivists, Jimmy had criminal entanglements dating back to early childhood. Upon leaving prison, with its forced discipline and rigidly manipulated control of both physical and social activities, he had returned to what had been, for him, a normal pattern of life.

But "normal" for Jimmy and "normal" for an employed, homeowning, churchgoing white- or blue-collar worker are totally different concepts. Jimmy had never worked regularly in his life; entering a job market where unemployment among adult whites was already over 10 per cent made finding work almost impossible. Yet a job was a condition of his parole! Through his mother's boy friend he managed to get work briefly as a warehouseman but was laid off after a few weeks. He shrugged off parole restrictions against drinking (abstinence being less normal than overindulgence among those he had known and associated with all of his life) and got into several fights (also a normal element in his background).

Both to increase his need for esteem among his friends and to have money to spend when he wanted it, Jimmy resumed the only vocation at which he had ever had any success. A series of burglaries preceded his armed robbery of several liquor stores, a gas station and an all-night market. He boasted about his "takes," and a bar hanger-on — an informer — turned him in. He was arrested, identified in a lineup and convicted on four of the five counts brought against him...

Criminology professor Mary G. Almore of the University of Texas at Arlington, in commenting on the superficial criticisms of rehabilitation by those favoring determinate sentences and the strict punishment of criminals, has observed; "Rehabilitation means to *restore* to useful, productive and acceptable... lives. How many residents of our prisons ever led particularly useful, productive and acceptable lives?"...

Behavioral counseling — including in-depth or group analysis — can alter an individual's attitudes and self-awareness, but it doesn't change the job market, the existence of ghettos or the ideas and ideals of those on the outside. A rehabilitation program centered on such counseling becomes an Oz lost by the prisoner as soon as he or she returns to the streets.

Even less successful at rehabilitating prisoners are "vocational programs" like those at Huntsville, Texas, where the major industry is the cutting and stamping of the state's license plates...

"AS YOU CAN SEE, WE HAVE COMPLETELY STREAMLINED OUR REHABILITATION PROGRAMS..."

Other state prison programs to which the designation "rehabilitative" is often attached include craft training (such as upholstering) in a geographic area where there is a "zero possibility" for employment in that field — or barber training in a state where felons cannot, by law, become licensed barbers. Even in those prisons where machine shop and heavy equipment or electronics training is available, the equipment often is so old that the practical value of the training is negated as a way of providing the prisoner trainee with a means of getting a job on the outside.

And those prisoners who do complete a fairly modernized vocational program of some kind are usually thrust directly into the job market to fend for themselves. "There's two kinds of people," an Ohio ex-con told me, "those that've been to prison and those that ain't. Once you been there, they don't never take it off your record." Despite high scores on several employment tests, this armed-robbery recidivist had been turned away from jobs because the companies involved did not hire felons. Like most ex-offenders, he was not eligible for bonding and could not get a contractor's (or any other) license because of his record.

Thus, his first four-year term (of which he served slightly less than two years) became a "life prison sentence."...

In both his case and Jimmy's, the problem of rehabilitation and adjustment centered not only on hesitance by employers to hire ex-offenders, but also on the ex-prisoners' inadequacies in returning to a society which judges its participants by material standards. Neither man was really prepared to find or hold a job (neither had had a record of steady employment before his incarceration). Each had been adequately punished, according to law, but neither could find a way to make it without resorting to crime...

LET'S GIVE REHABILITATION A CHANCE

Bucking the groundswell of support for punishment as opposed to rehabilitation will do neither prisoners nor reform-minded penologists any good. On the other hand, programs that would bring a felon out of prison into a job he or she can handle might enable the prison system to reduce recidivism dramatically.

A first step would be to separate the "punishment" from the "rehabilitative" stages of sentencing. The former would consist of a strict and definite term that could not be significantly reduced by parole. The latter would involve comprehensive job training in fields that would be open to the newly trained ex-con immediately upon release. "The prison labor force is grossly underutilized, which is a loss to society and to the individuals," states Robert Taggart III in *The Prison of Unemployment*.

Work-release and work-furlough programs in some states enable convicted drunk drivers and others to continue to hold jobs while spending their nights and weekends in jail. Similar services are sometimes available to offenders being programmed out of prison. But very little has been done to integrate training, job search and ongoing employment. Few state prison systems have attempted to coordinate the release of prisoners with active employment in private industry. (Those ex-prisoners who do find jobs are often the first to be laid off during a slowdown, and they frequently drift back into crime.) Parole officers and judges are often at a loss to understand why an ex-con can't "go out and get a job and work like everybody else."

As Mary Almore pointed out, the question is not so much one of "rehabilitation" as it is of beginning a new way of life. Taggart claims that the most effective rehabilitation for first- and second-time offenders involves presentencing intervention. The job program is set up before the subject leaves the courtroom and continues to prepare the individual for release while he or she is in prison.

Were such programs more widespread, both the "punishment" aspect and the needs for rehabilitation could be satisfied. The institutional churches of the United States could play a much stronger social role in the life of the community by helping to develop organized job programs. Many ex-convicts might be diverted from recidivism if they had community backing in the form of temporary employment, skill training and problem-solving resources when they are first threatened with lay-off or when they lose or quit a job.

Prison-initiated projects could be established for older recidivists at lower cost than that of most prison maintenance programs. Before such programs could be implemented, however, the "Huntsville philosophy" of cheap — virtually slave — labor must be displaced, and a responsible course charted so that those behind bars who will try to make it on the outside stand a better chance of doing so.

Until there is a place in our social system for the human products of our prisons, ex-convicts will continue to support themselves through violence, and we, the victims, will go on deepening the trench between us and those who need more than a Freudian mind-shaking to counterbalance lives of crime.

DETERMINING PRISONERS' RIGHTS

Examine the following list of prisoners' rights. It was compiled by a group of people who are former prisoners, relatives of prisoners or individuals who have a lot of contact with prisoners. This group of Quakers and non-Quakers organized to study prisons and submit proposals to improve them. They called their proposals for reform a *Prisoners Bill of Rights*.

Many people would agree with these proposals and many would disagree. What do you think?

Examine the following proposals carefully. Mark *A* for proposals you agree with. Mark *D* for proposals you disagree with. Mark *C* for proposals you think are too complex to judge. Then compare your choices with other class members.

> A = Proposals you agree with
> D = Proposals you disagree with
> C = Proposals too complex to judge

PRISONERS BILL OF RIGHTS

_____ 1. Freedom from abuse or threat of abuse from custodial personnel or prisoners.

_____ 2. Uninterrupted access to legal and psychological counseling.

_____ 3. Adequate diet and sanitation, fresh air, exercise, medical treatment, and prescription drugs.

_____ 4. Regular contact through meetings or correspondence with family, close friends, public officials and concerned organizations.

The Prisoners Bill of Rights is taken from *Prisons: Criminal Injustice — Working Party Studies Alternatives* by the American Friends Service Committee and *The Problem of Prisons* by David F. Greenberg.

_____ 5. Regular periods of unprogrammed time.

_____ 6. Welfare payments on release from prison.

_____ 7. Exclusive title to and control over all products of literary, artistic, or personal craftsmanship produced on his own time.

_____ 8. Periodic review of a prisoner's case by an impartial outside authority with the power to offer probation or commutation of the sentence.

_____ 9. The full restoration of all civil rights and privileges on termination of parole.

_____ 10. Prisoners should be entitled to all civil liberties guaranteed by the constitution, including the right to unlimited, uncensored correspondence with anyone, the right to receive any books, magazines or newspapers, to receive visits from anyone, the right to publish articles, and to hold political meetings in prison. These rights would help reduce the power an administration has over inmates, and above all, will allow him to publicize conditions in the prison.

_____ 11. Prisoners should be entitled to all rights of due process for infraction of prison regulations.

_____ 12. No prisoner should be forced to work.

_____ 13. Each prisoner should be entitled to a monthly cash allowance to pay travel expenses for friends and relatives who wish to visit.

_____ 14. A prisoner should be able to see and to insert material in the records kept on him by the prison administration. This is important because negative reports inserted by the administration in his record may jeopardize his chances at parole.

_____ 15. Prisoners should have the right of conjugal visits or furloughs at frequent intervals, from spouses or other men or women.

_____ 16. Prisoners are entitled to educational and vocational training programs consistent with their interests. When these are not available inside the prisons, the inmate must be allowed to participate in such programs either through correspondence courses or through study and work training programs outside the prison at government expense.

_____ List other proposals you think should be included.

107

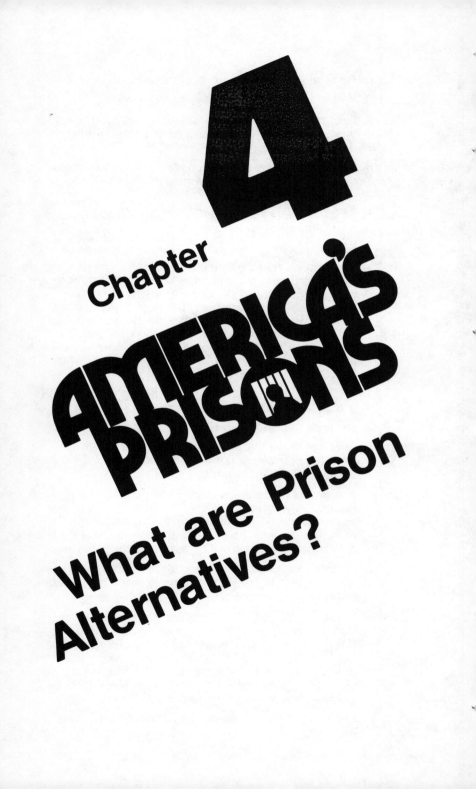

Chapter

4

AMERICA'S PRISONS

What are Prison Alternatives?

*"If the prisons were opened
tomorrow, it wouldn't make any
difference. The fear of crime is a
greater problem than crime itself."*

WHY PUT PEOPLE IN PRISONS?

Robert A. Fangmeier

Mr. Fangmeier recently took early retirement after 22 years on
the staff of the Division of Homeland Ministries, Christian
Church (Disciples of Christ).

Consider the following questions while reading:
1. *Are we safer because prisoners are behind bars,
   according to the author?*
2. *What types of prisoners would not need imprisonment,
   according to Mr. Fangmeier?*
3. *In the author's view, about what percentage of prisoners
   really need to be incarcerated?*
4. *How would the poor benefit by a bail-bond reform?*

Robert A. Fangmeier, "Myths and Realities About Prisons and Jails,"
Copyright 1980 Christian Century Foundation. Reprinted by permission from
the March 19, 1980 issue of *The Christian Century*, pp. 324-25.

ONLY A FEW GO TO PRISON

If the idea of prison abolition at first seems a bit impractical even to liberals, it becomes somewhat more plausible as the ideology is examined in juxtaposition with strategy and tactics...

Hans Mattick, criminologist, has this to say to the fearful: "If the prisons were opened tomorrow, it wouldn't make any difference. The fear of crime is a greater problem than crime itself." He explains that for every 100 serious crimes reported, there are 25 arrests and 12 convictions with only three imprisonments. He doesn't think the release of the three would make much difference in the crime rate. Mattick's thesis is supported by the President's Commission on Causes and Prevention of Violence, which estimated that "only 1.5 per cent of the perpetrators of the approximately 9 million crimes committed annually end up in prison."

The awareness that only a minuscule number of law violators go to prison at least raises serious questions about the prevailing mythology that we are significantly safer because several hundred thousand people are behind bars. It sets the stage for several other questions: Why are these people incarcerated? Who are they? And is their interest and ours better served by their imprisonment?

PRISON PROFILE

As a beginning point in the search for answers to these questions, a profile of the prison and jail population is instructive. Those incarcerated are largely from minority groups and the poor. Jesse Jackson, director of Operation PUSH, estimates that of the approximately 400,000 persons being held in American jails and prisons, 300,000 are either black or brown. A typical example that confirms Jackson's estimate is the infamous Attica Prison in New York at the time of the 1973 massacre. Blacks and Spanish-speaking inmates made up 70 per cent of the population.

The poor and the minorities also account for nearly all of the 50,000 people in county jails on an average day as pretrial detainees. They are there because of an archaic bail-bond system that favors the professional criminal (who counts bail as a business expense) and the affluent. Despite pious constitutional prohibitions against "excessive bail," all bail is excessive to those who cannot afford it. Bail was designed to assure the defendant's appearance in court. That is its only constitutional purpose. It has, however, been distorted into a weapon of discrimination used against the poor, who tend to show up for trial as readily as their more affluent neighbors.

VICTIMLESS CRIMES

Another large bloc in the inmate population consists of those involved in so-called "victimless crimes." *U.S. News and World Report* has calculated that these offenses account for $20 billion of our $51 billion annual crime bill. The best-known example is the annual figure of 2 million arrests for drunkenness. This constitutes the largest single category of all arrests — somewhere between one-fourth and one-third, and approximately one-half of all convictions.

The arrest of drunks is a costly, counterproductive and demeaning response to an illness. One survey showed that six men had been arrested a total of 1,409 times and served 125 years in jail, at a cost of $600,000 to the taxpayers. If vagrancy and loitering charges are combined with those for drunkenness, the total reaches about 3 million annually. The half-million marijuana arrests annually, constituting 70 per cent of all drug-related arrests, fall into the same category of "victimless crimes" which many reformers believe should be decriminalized. To the extent that these victimless activities are a matter of public concern, they require medical treatment, income-maintenance and education. Imprisonment benefits neither the inmate nor the public.

If the prisons were opened tomorrow it wouldn't make any difference.

ALTERNATIVES FOR NONVIOLENT OFFENDERS

The genuine fear felt by the public is associated with violent crime. Those who seek alternatives to prisons and jails understand this. They recognize that there are some in our society who must for their own good and ours be institutionalized. These people account for no more than one-fourth of all prisoners, and some estimates put the figure as low as 10 per cent. It is an underexplored and underfunded area where treatment rather than imprisonment could produce beneficial results. In any event, the separation of violent from nonviolent prisoners can make the idea of "alternatives to prison" more palatable.

The alternatives are familiar enough when we view the prison and jail population from another angle. White-collar criminals are usually big-timers in terms of the gross annual larceny take from the public. But they are nonviolent, their activities are distant from the average citizen's experience, and therefore they are less feared. They include public officials, embezzlers and those convicted of consumer fraud. Their "status" makes imprisonment less likely. Alternatives to imprisonment seem acceptable in these circumstances.

Only 18 per cent of the embezzlers, for example, end up in prison, but nearly all bank thieves who use a gun are put behind bars if they are apprehended. The size of the take matters little, but the method does. If violence or potential violence is to be the dividing line, it is interesting to compare the nonviolent embezzler with the nonviolent auto thief. Whereas less than a fifth of the embezzlers go to prison, over two-thirds of car thieves do. The majority of the white-collar criminals get suspended sentences or probation; they also may pay fines and take part in programs of restitution to their victims. The nonviolent poor rarely are offered these non-prison alternatives as a way of paying their debt to society.

In addition, so far as the public is concerned, imprisonment offers potential victims short-term security at best. Ninety-five per cent of those incarcerated are released after serving an average sentence of from 24 to 32 months. With rare exceptions, they are less likely than those not imprisoned to adjust to normal legal social patterns. This should not be surprising. The prisoner has lived in an atmosphere of distrust and violence that tends to exacerbate existing antisocial attitudes. An ex-convict comes home with few marketable skills and a prison record that is a barrier to any stable employment.

ALTERNATIVES THAT WORK

Alternatives to prison and jail have long been available to certain classes of criminals and are increasingly being pilot-tested for others. The Des Moines program is an example of a growing nationwide movement for bail-bond reform. In a five-year period it produced a 95 per cent show-up-at-trial rate in securing the release of 3,800 poor defendants. It equaled the show-up rate of those set free on money bond or their own recognizance. The county and state saved money in prison costs, family welfare benefits and tax revenues since the pre-trial defendants could work. Counseling was provided in such areas as family life, employment, alcoholism and law. The success of the project led to a decision to shut down two maximum-security institutions and to use the money saved to duplicate the program throughout Iowa.

In Massachusetts all juvenile institutions were closed out over a three-year period. The young people were sent home or to alternative projects, depending on circumstances. In this instance an enlightened administrator used federal funds (LEAA) to engineer the abolition of all juvenile institutions in the state. As a result, the negative effects of incarceration were replaced by a positive thrust to prepare the young people to return to school or the workaday world.

Georgia, Alabama, Florida and California are examples of states where court orders forced the early release of inmates, with positive results. Because of overcrowding, the first two states were held to be in violation of the Constitution's "cruel and unusual punishment" clause. In California the issue was the arbitrary administration of indeterminate sentences which invariably led to the longest possible term. Florida had to give early release to 1,252 poor felons who were convicted without counsel.

The awareness that only a minuscule number of law violators go to prison at least raises serious questions about the prevailing mythology that we are significantly safer because several hundred thousand people are behind bars.

The postprison experience of the Florida inmates is typical of other men and women released early. They had a recidivism rate of only 13.6 per cent, compared to 25 per cent for those who served their full time. The early-release people adjusted better on the outside and helped to puncture the myth that longer sentences are better for the community.

"Would you rather be subjected to a few minutes of intense pain and considerable public humiliation, or be locked away for two or three years in a prison cell crowded with ill-tempered sociopaths?"

CAN WE LEARN FROM EASTERN CULTURES?

Stephen Chapman

Stephen Chapman is a 1976 Graduate of Harvard University. He has written for a number of magazines including, *Harpers*, *Fortune*, *Public Interest*, *TV-Guide* and *The New Republic* in which the following viewpoint appeared.

Consider the following questions while reading:
1. **How does punishment in Eastern cultures differ from punishment in the West?**
2. **How does the author describe "the advantages of being a convicted criminal in an advanced culture"?**
3. **What does the author list as the five goals of imprisonment?**
4. **Which system of justice do you think is most barbaric?**

Stephen Chapman, "The Prisoner's Dilemma," *The New Republic*, March 8, 1980, pp. 20-23. Reprinted by permission of THE NEW REPUBLIC, © 1980, The New Republic, Inc.

PUNISHMENT IN EASTERN CULTURES

One of the amusements of life in the modern West is the opportunity to observe the barbaric rituals of countries that are attached to the customs of the dark ages. Take Pakistan, for example, our newest ally and client state in Asia. Last October President Zia, in harmony with the Islamic fervor that is sweeping his part of the world, revived the traditional Moslem practice of flogging lawbreakers in public. In Pakistan, this qualified as mass entertainment, and no fewer than 10,000 law-abiding Pakistanis turned out to see justice done to 26 convicts. To Western sensibilities the spectacle seemed barbaric — both in the sense of cruel and in the sense of pre-civilized. In keeping with Islamic custom each of the unfortunates — who had been caught in prostitution raids the previous night and summarily convicted and sentenced — was stripped down to a pair of white shorts, which were painted with a red stripe across the buttocks (the target). Then he was shackled against an easel, with pads thoughtfully placed over the kidneys to prevent injury. The floggers were muscular, fierce-looking sorts — convicted murderers, as it happens — who paraded around the flogging platform in colorful loincloths. When the time for the ceremony began, one of the floggers took a running start and brought a five-foot stave down across the first victim's buttocks, eliciting screams from the convict and murmurs from the audience. Each of the 26 received from five to 15 lashes. One had to be carried from the stage unconscious.

Flogging is one of the punishments stipulated by Koranic law, which has made it a popular penological device in several Moslem countries, including Pakistan, Saudi Arabia, and, most recently, the ayatollah's Iran. Flogging, or *ta'zir*, is the general punishment prescribed for offenses that don't carry an explicit Koranic penalty. Some crimes carry automatic *hadd* punishments — stoning or scourging (a severe whipping) for illicit sex, scourging for drinking alcoholic beverages, amputation of the hands for theft. Other crimes — as varied as murder and abandoning Islam — carry the death penalty (usually carried out in public)...

Such traditions, we all must agree, are no sign of an advanced civilization. In the West, we have replaced these various punishments (including the death penalty in most cases) with a single device. Our custom is to confine criminals in prison for varying lengths of time...

115

WHICH SYSTEM IS
MORE BARBARIC?

PUNISHMENT IN THE WEST

The punishment *intended* by Western societies in sending their criminals to prison is the loss of freedom. But, as everyone knows, the actual punishment in most American prisons is of a wholly different order. The February 2 riot at New Mexico's state prison in Santa Fe, one of several bloody prison riots in the nine years since the Attica bloodbath, once again dramatized the conditions of life in an American prison. Four hundred prisoners seized control of the prison before dawn. By sunset the next day 33 inmates had died at the hands of other convicts and another 40 people (including five guards) had been seriously hurt. Macabre stories came out of prisoners being hanged, murdered with blowtorches, decapitated, tortured, and mutilated in a variety of gruesome ways by drug-crazed rioters.

Perhaps it sounds barbaric to talk of flogging and amputation, and perhaps it is. But our system of punishment also is barbaric, and probably more so.

The Santa Fe penitentiary was typical of most maximum-security facilities, with prisoners subject to overcrowding, filthy conditions, and routine violence. It also housed first-time, non-violent offenders, like check forgers and drug dealers, with murderers serving life sentences. In a recent lawsuit, the American Civil Liberties Union called the prison "totally unfit for human habitation." But the ACLU says New Mexico's pentitentiary is far from the nation's worst...

What are the advantages of being a convicted criminal in an advanced culture? First there is the overcrowding in prisons. One Tennessee prison, for example, has a capacity of 806, according to accepted space standards, but it houses 2300 inmates. One Louisiana facility has confined four and five prisoners in a single six-foot-by-six-foot cell. Then there is the disease caused by overcrowding, unsanitary conditions, and poor or inadequate medical care. A federal appeals court noted that the Tennessee prison had suffered frequent outbreaks of infectious diseases like hepatitis and tuberculosis. But the most distinctive element of American prison life is its

WHIPPING THE CRIMINAL

Flogging is alive and well today in Singapore, and police officials in that Asian city-state say it deters crime. Singapore is considered virtually free of street crime. Corporal punishment, inherited from the British in colonial days, was retained after independence in 1963 with a local refinement. A thin rod of ratan — a "rotan" — is used in officially prescribed whippings. A hard blow splits the skin, draws blood and leaves a scar.

"Caning helps to restrain a vicious thug from committing physical violence and imposes a stigma on those who have been caned," Singapore's deputy police commissioner was quoted as saying in The Wall Street Journal, *July 6, 1977. The newspaper reported that Singapore experimented with milder forms of punishment in the 1960s but a rise in crime prompted the parliament to rewrite the penal code, spelling out the number of "rotan" strokes for each offense. Armed robbery, for instance, draws a minimum of 10 strokes.*

In the United States, corporal punishment was practiced in some prisons until the Supreme Court outlawed it in 1968. But in April 1977 the court upheld its use in schools in some circumstances.

From *Crime and Justice* by Editorial Research Reports, 1978.

constant violence. In his book *Criminal Violence, Criminal Justice*, Charles Silberman noted that in one Louisiana prison, there were 211 stabbings in only three years, 11 of them fatal. There were 15 slayings in a prison in Massachusetts between 1972 and 1975. According to a federal court, in Alabama's penitentiaries (as in many others), "robbery, rape, extortion, theft and assault are everyday occurrences."

At least in regard to cruelty, it's not at all clear that the system of punishment that has evolved in the West is less barbaric than the grotesque practices of Islam. Skeptical? Ask yourself: would you rather be subjected to a few minutes of intense pain and considerable public humiliation, or to be locked away for two or three years in a prison cell crowded with ill-tempered sociopaths? Would you rather lose a hand or spend 10 years or more in a typical state prison? I have taken my own survey on this matter. I have found no one who does not find the Islamic system hideous. And I have found no one who, given the choices mentioned above, would not prefer its penalties to our own...

THE 5 GOALS OF IMPRISONMENT

Imprisonment is now the universal method of punishing criminals in the United States. It is thought to perform five functions, each of which has been given a label by criminologists. First, there is simple *retribution:* punishing the lawbreaker to serve society's sense of justice and to satisfy the victims' desire for revenge. Second, there is *specific deterrence:* discouraging the offender from misbehaving in the future. Third, *general deterrence:* using the offender as an example to discourage others from turning to crime. Fourth, *prevention:* at least during the time he is kept off the streets, the criminal cannot victimize other members of society. Finally, and most important, there is *rehabilitation:* reforming the criminal so that when he returns to society he will be inclined to obey the laws and able to make an honest living.

How satisfactorily do American prisons perform by these criteria? Well, of course, they do punish. But on the other scores they don't do so well. Their effect in discouraging future criminality by the prisoner or others is the subject of much debate, but the soaring rates of the last 20 years suggest that prisons are not a dramatically effective deterrent to criminal behavior. Prisons do isolate convicted criminals, but only to divert crime from ordinary citizens to prison guards and fellow inmates. Almost no one contends anymore that prisons rehabilitate their inmates. If anything, they probably impede rehabilitation by forcing inmates into prolonged and almost exclusive association with other criminals...

No one, of course, would think of copying the medieval practices of Islamic nations and experimenting with punishments such as flogging and amputation. But let us consider them anyway. How do they compare with our American prison system in achieving the ostensible objectives of punishment? First, do they punish? Obviously they do, and in a uniquely painful and memorable way...Do they deter crime? Yes, and probably more effectively than sending convicts off to prison...

Do flogging and amputation discourage recidivism? No one knows whether the scars on his back would dissuade a criminal from risking another crime, but it is hard to imagine that corporal measures could stimulate a higher rate of recidivism than already exists...

Do these medieval forms of punishment rehabilitate the criminal? Plainly not. But long prison terms do not rehabilitate either...

Of course there are other reasons besides its bizarre forms of punishment that the Islamic system of justice seems uncivilized to the Western mind. One is the absence of due process... The vast majority of American criminals are convicted and sentenced as a result of plea bargaining, in which due process plays almost no role...Finally, my lawyer friends assure me that the rules of jurisdiction for American courts contain plenty of petty requirements and bizarre distinctions that would sound silly enough to foreign ears.

To choose imprisonment over flogging and amputation is not to choose human kindness over cruelty, but merely to prefer that our cruelties be kept out of sight, and out of mind.

Perhaps it sounds barbaric to talk of flogging and amputation, and perhaps it is. But our system of punishment also is barbaric, and probably more so. Only cultural smugness about their system and willful ignorance about our own make it easy to regard the one as cruel and the other as civilized. We inflict our cruelties away from public view, while nations like Pakistan stage them in front of 10,000 onlookers. Their outrages are visible; ours are not. Most Americans can live their lives for years without having their peace of mind disturbed by the knowledge of what goes on in our prisons. To choose imprisonment over flogging and amputation is not to choose human kindness over cruelty, but merely to prefer that our cruelties be kept out of sight, and out of mind.

ALTERNATIVE 3

"Probation is a sentence under which convicted offenders are released with their promise to be good and to accept supervision."

PROBATION INSTEAD OF PRISON

Austin C. Wehrwein

Austin Wehrwein is an editorial writer for the *Minneapolis Star*. He has a law degree from Columbia University. In 1953 he won a Pulitzer Prize for a series of newspaper articles on an economic survey of Canada.

Consider the following questions while reading:
1. What conclusions about probation does the author make on the basis of the Arkansas study?
2. Why does this viewpoint claim probation is often more effective than imprisonment? Do you agree?
3. What problems does the author cite in using probation?
4. How does probation differ from parole?

From Austin C. Wehrwein, "Probation Concept Receives Support In New Studies," *The Minneapolis Star*. October 5, 1979. Reprinted with permission.

I recently received a letter from Judge Gerald W. Heaney of the Eighth Circuit Court of Appeals, which sits in St. Louis, and whose writ runs in seven states — from the top of Minnesota to the end of Nebraska and down to Arkansas.

Heaney, whose year-round home and office are in Duluth, enclosed a report on how probation has worked in one of the Arkansas federal judicial districts. Heaney commented that it shows there's very little recidivism (few repeaters) among adequately supervised first-time offenders. He added:

"I really have a lot of misgivings about the directions that sentencing is taking, both at the state and federal levels." He's concerned with the hard-line attitude that more people should be imprisoned and for longer times.

COMMUNITY BASED CORRECTIONS

The present era of corrections is focusing on community corrections in the belief that programs in the community can be more productive in changing patterns of crime than traditional incarceration with its higher rate of failure.

In the Federal courts, the use of probation has steadily increased until slightly more than half of all convicted persons are placed on probation. Federal probation services have been productive as evidenced by the fact that currently more than 80 percent of probationers complete supervision without violation and more than 70 percent of Federal parolees are terminated successfully.

The cost of supervision of a person on probation averages one-tenth that of imprisonment. Taxpayer savings occur when offenders on probation remain at liberty to work, support their families, and pay their fair share of the taxes. Yet economics is only one issue. It is through probation that the offender is reconciled with his community and for this reason community supervision offers greater promise for a reduction in the rate of crime.

From a Federal Bureau of Prisons pamphlets titled Where It Counts: Lives in the Balance. Distributed in 1980.

The study was prepared for the U.S. District Court for the Eastern District of Arkansas by the district's probation office, Heaney was reflecting on the report's key decision:

"Is probation a worthwhile alternative to incarceration (imprisonment)? Our conclusion is an emphatic 'Yes,' both economically and socially. Economically, incarceration [costs] *ten times*...probation. Socially, the probationer can remain within his family structure, thereby providing economic security to his family; and, with proper rehabilitative efforts, he can become a productive citizen."

The report's key statistic is the success rate: 84.1 percent of a sample of 126 probationers stayed out of serious trouble during a five-year period, 1970-75. In other words, four out of five who beat the slammer rap really were good risks...

The public tends to confuse probation and parole. Both have, in any event, been the target of the critics who charge that, either way, criminals are turned loose to prey on more victims.

To be precise, probation is a sentence under which *convicted* offenders are released with their promise to be good and to accept supervision...

In contrast, parole is granted, also with conditions, *after* a convicted criminal has served some time behind bars. The word comes from the French, *parole d'honneur*, or "word of honor." New York state started the first regular parole system in 1871. In any case, what this column is about is probation. As I see it, the theory underlying probation is that arrest, trial and conviction are, for many, punishment enough. Lots of people won't buy that theory, but it does meet one test of criminal law — deterrence. Merely being in the soup once will make many people vow to go straight forever. (Especially if they know they're being checked up on.)

Anyhow, good or bad, probation is, in fact, the most frequent sentence handed out nationally. Experts tell me that, if anything, probation will become even more prevalent. In Minnesota today there are about 2,000 adult criminals incarcerated, about 7,400 on parole and 3,700 on probation. The experts also tell me that the best study available in Minnesota was released last year by the Hennepin County Court Services' District Court Probation Division.

Although the study used a one-year follow-up period as opposed to the five years used in Arkansas, the overall success rate reported here was 84.3 percent, or virtually identical with the Arkansas figure. Both, by the way, focused on new felony convictions. On the other hand, when all convictions are counted — including felonies, misdemeanors and technical violations of probation conditions — the Hennepin County success rate was still about 77 percent.

THE AMERICAN CORRECTIONAL ASSOCIATION

The American Correctional Association endorses probation as a realistic alternative to incarceration as a sentencing disposition by the Courts for juvenile and adult offenders...

Placement of offenders back into the community allows for access to available treatment programs, continued support for the family through gainful employment, the availability to maintain family ties, academic opportunities, restitution reimbursement, counseling, and community services in lieu of institutionalization. This assistance will promote a socially acceptable lifestyle, while simultaneously monitoring the offender's behavior to assure conformity to the law and the stipulated conditions of release.

A savings to the taxpayer is accomplished when the possibility exists to consider a sentence to probation.

If attempts to accomplish these goals fail, incarceration becomes appropriate.

The American Correctional Association adopted this position in 1978.

Put it all together and you can make a case that probation can indeed work, even allowing for the differences between federal and state criminal law and between Arkansas and Minnesota. But even a nonexpert can come up with some "Yes, buts." One is that success will hinge on whether there are enough skilled probation officers to cope with the swelling ranks of probationers. Typically, critics say that probation officers are few, badly trained and swamped with work. Second, by definition, for goodness sake, a probationer *is* a reasonably good risk. If he or she weren't, he or she would go to the joint. And, sure enough, the figures show that the better the risk the less the recidivism.

124

Still, if you wanted to argue not only that probation can be made to work but there should be more of it, a position with which Judge Heaney would evidentially agree, you'd find useful guidelines in the Arkansas study. For example, blacks and women are as good risks as white males. Nor did it make any difference whether the probationers (below age 28) were poorer risks than older. Those with prior criminal records, especially if they had done time, are worse risks than first offenders. The first eight months "on the street" are the most critical period of adjustment.

"Recidivism appears to be strongly influenced by lack of formal education," the report said. "It was also evident that recidivism is primarily an urban problem. An additional revelation was that the majority of those reverting to criminal activity become involved in *an identical or similar offense* as the one for which they were placed on probation."

"It has long been Swedish policy to avoid the use of imprisonment as much as possible and more and more importance is attached to the use of non-institutional measures."

A LOOK AT SWEDISH PRISONS

Swedish National Prison & Probation Administration

The following viewpoint was taken from the 1978 annual report of the Swedish National Prison and Probation Administration..

Consider the following questions while reading:
1. What are the basic principles of Swedish prison policy?
2. How are Swedish offenders assigned to prisons?
3. What work and educational programs are available to Swedish prisoners?
4. How is the Swedish probationer supervised?
5. What is the difference between open and closed local institutions?

REFORM OF THE PRISON AND PROBATION SYSTEM

Of major importance for the correctional system's work since 1974 has been the implementation of a far-reaching reorganization of the system...

The basic principles are as follows. The importance of handling offenders without deprivation of liberty is emphasized. Where deprivation of liberty is unavoidably necessary it should be organized so as to keep the offender in close contact with society. To that end offenders serving sentences of up to one year, i.e. about 90 per cent of the early intake, are to be sent to small institutions in their own localities. Only offenders serving longer terms will be allocated to national prisons but these too can be admitted to local institutions for the terminal phase of sentence. The local institutions are intended to have open, flexible regimes which will permit inmates to have intensive contact with normal society and especially with families, employers, educational facilities and leisure time associations. Preparation for release must be started in good time. Responsibility for this lies with the local probation office. A further principle is that prisoners do not forfeit their right to use the various social service agencies by reason of their sentence and therefore the community's social service bodies should be utilized whenever necessary...With the aim of increasing effectiveness in probation and parole work, a steady increase in professional staff has taken place...

INSTITUTIONAL ALLOCATION

The allocation of prisoners to an appropriate establishment is ordinarily the responsibility of the regional director assisted by the members of a treatment board. Both prison and probation staff take part. As explained earlier, the Act on Correctional Treatment in Institutions requires that prisoners be assigned to institutions near their homes or in the case of longer term prisoners, should serve the terminal phase in a local institution. Consideration is also given to other factors including the need to provide vocational training, education or some special treatment.

WORK PROGRAMS

Institutional treatment implies a policy of full employment. Every able-bodied man who can work a normal 40-hour week is required to do so. The sole exceptions are for persons awaiting trial and the ill or disabled.

About 2,500 openings are available in industry and 700 in mechanized farming and forestry. There are also simpler tasks in cells (chiefly for persons awaiting trial) and maintenance duties available to some extent.

The workshops at the new institutions are fully comparable in every respect with their counterparts in civilian life. Even the older institutions seek to organize their work programs in accordance with present-day manufacturing principles.

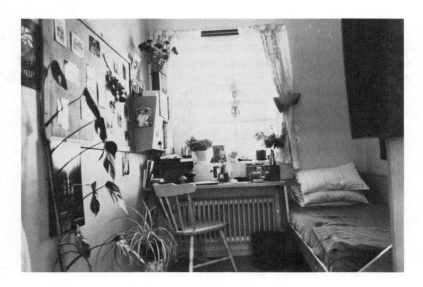

A CELL IN HINSEBERG, A CLOSED NATIONAL PRISON FOR FEMALE OFFENDERS

Emphasis in the manufacturing sector is on iron, steel and wood products together with the production of clothing. Some institutions specialize in plastics while others run large scale laundries. Building and construction is another important industry.

All work is remunerated, with piece-rates used wherever possible...

Besides the activities inside the institutions the Act on Correctional Treatment in Institutions provides greater opportunities for the granting of permits to inmates for special activities outside the institution. Such permits allow the inmate of an institution to work or participate in schooling, training or other specially arranged activities, e.g. study excursions, outside the institution during working hours. These permits are intended chiefly for inmates of local institutions, but if there are special reasons for doing so they can be granted to inmates of national institutions...

SENTENCES TO IMPRISONMENT

In 1978 10,547 persons sentenced to imprisonment were admitted to correctional institutions.

About 68 per cent of the newcomers were sentenced to less than four months' deprivation of liberty and eleven per cent to one year or more.

The admitted persons are distributed by principal offense as follows:

Driving whilst intoxicated	34 per cent
Larceny	20 per cent
Violence	14 per cent
Fraud	4 per cent
Drug Act	4 per cent
Insubordination	2 per cent
Aliens' Act	3 per cent
Other	19 per cent
of which with two or more equally serious offences in the judgement rendered	*10 per cent*
Registered	100 per cent

FURLOUGHS

Under the Act on Correctional Treatment in Institutions the rules for furlough have been made less restrictive. An inmate may be granted permission to leave an institution for a specified brief period in order to facilitate his adjustment in society (short furlough) as long as there is no considerable risk for misuse. As preparation for release prisoners can also be given the opportunity of living outside the institution even before the date of release (release furlough)...

Altogether 41,974 furloughs were approved in 1978. Of these 2,601 (6 per cent) were abused in the sense that the inmate did not return to the institution within the time allowed and 1,170 (3 per cent) due to other misconduct, e.g. misuse of alcohol or narcotics or criminal activities.

ROSTUNA, AN OPEN LOCAL PRISON

NON-INSTITUTIONAL TREATMENT

It has long been Swedish policy to avoid the use of imprison-ment as much as possible and more and more importance is attached to the use of non-institutional measures. The number of persons sentenced to the sanction of probation was 6,634 in 1978. In the same year the total number of persons under probation supervision was 13,239. In addition to these probationers, a further 3,004 persons, were under supervision as parolees from youth prisons, ordinary prisons and the special internment prisons.

It is a distincitve feature of probation and parole work that it is undertaken by only a small number of professional fulltime probation officers who are supported by about 9,000 auxiliary workers. It is the latter who take much of the personal contact work with clients. Caseloads are therefore small, with most voluntary workers having no more than one or two cases. The professional probation officers are mainly organizers and counsellors although of course some of the more difficult cases require their special direct attention...

RECIDIVISM

The National Central Bureau of Statistics publishes reports on recidivism. Recidivism is defined as relapse into crime carrying more serious penalties than fines alone. The relapse must have been recorded as a result of a court decision or a prosecutor's decision to waive prosecution.

TOILET FACILITIES IN A CELL AT HELSINBORG, AN OPEN LOCAL PRISON

For those sentenced in 1972 and at the risk for the following three years the relapse rates are as follows. For prison sentences of 1-4 months the rates for those without previous convictions and with previous convictions were 15 per cent and 44 per cent respectively. For first offenders sentenced to imprisonment for five months or more, the relapse rate was 19 per cent. The corresponding rate for those with previous convictions was 67 per cent.

LOCAL INSTITUTIONS

The inmtes' living quarters are arranged in eight groups of five rooms each. This makes for a quieter atmosphere in the institution and also allows some differentiation to be made among categories of inmates. Each local institution has at least two places for female inmates in an accommodation section separate from the rest. The institution also has a kitchen and a common dining room for inmates and staff. There are showers in each section for the use of the inmates, and also a sauna and laundry.

SECURITY ARRANGEMENTS

Some of the new local institutions are to be of open type and others closed. In the closed local institutions measures are taken to prevent inmates escaping and also to prevent prohibited types of contact with the outside world, such as the smuggling of liquor and narcotics. For this reason they are surrounded by a double wire-netting fence three meters high and fitted with windows of unbreakable glass. Inmates who behave violently or disruptively may be temporarily confined in two observation rooms located apart from the other living quarters. If an inmate persists in misbehaving he is transferred to a national institution. Alarm installations are provided for the safety of staff.

For those with previous offences who were sentenced to youth imprisonment — and this means the bulk of the youth prison population — the relapse rate was 84 per cent.

DISTINGUISHING BETWEEN STATEMENTS THAT ARE PROVABLE AND THOSE THAT ARE NOT

From various sources of information we are constantly confronted with statements and generalizations about social problems. In order to think clearly about these problems, it is useful if one can make a basic distinction between statements for which evidence can be found, and other statements which cannot be verified because evidence is not available, or the issue is so controversial that it cannot be definitely proved. Students should constantly be aware that social studies texts and other publications often contain statements of a controversial nature. The following activity is designed to allow you to experiment with statements that are provable and those that are not.

Read each of the following statements. Indicate whether you believe it is provable P, *too controversial to be proved to most people's satisfaction C,* or *unprovable because of the lack of evidence U.*

P = Provable
C = Too Controversial
U = Unprovable

_____ 1. Every prison system, must, of its very nature, be oppressive.

_____ 2. Prisoners have a right to a minimum wage.

_____ 3. Every federal prison is designed to provide training and treatment programs that meet the needs of each inmate.

_____ 4. Poor people commit more crimes than rich people.

_____ 5. Prison rapes are not a serious problem.

_____ 6. The United States has a better prison system than the countries of Western Europe.

_____ 7. Property offenses constitute about 90 percent of all crimes committed.

_____ 8. The Federal Bureau of Prisons pioneered improved living conditions for prison inmates.

_____ 9. Poverty is the cause of most crime.

_____ 10. Criminals could be rehabilitated more easily if society were not prejudiced against them.

_____ 11. Prisoners are sometimes victimized by guards.

_____ 12. Prison policies should be based mainly on economic considerations.

_____ 13. Allowing married prisoners to have conjugal rights would create more problems than it would solve.

ORGANIZATIONS TO CONTACT

Listed below are groups that were founded to deal with prison related problems. If you become interested in prisons you may want to contact these organizations for information or subscribe to their publications. You can find the names and addresses of additional groups in the *Encyclopedia of Associations* in the section "Corrections". Your school or local library should have this reference book.

American Civil Liberties Union Foundation Prison Project
Suite 1031
1346 Connecticut Ave., N.W.
Washington, D.C. 20036
Studies prison conditions and lobbies for change.

American Correctional Association
4321 Hartwick Rd.
College Park, MD 20740
Members are prison wardens and other prison officials and persons involved in corrections. Publishes Corrections Today.

The Angolite
Louisiana State Prison
Angola, LA 70712
Perhaps the best inmate publication in the country.

Federal Bureau of Prisons
320 First St., N.W.
Washington, D.C. 20534

The Fortune Society
229 Park Ave. South
New York, NY 10003
Composed of ex-convicts and others interested in penal reform.

Interreligious Taskforce On Criminal Justice
Room 1700
475 Riverside Drive
New York, NY 10027
An agency of both Protestants and Catholics working on criminal justice question.

National Council On Crime and Delinquency
411 Hackensack Ave.
Hackensack, NJ 07601

Perhaps the most prestigious criminal justice reform group in the country. Founded in 1907.

National Moratorium On Prison Construction
324 C Street, S.E.
Washington, D.C. 20003

Seeks alternatives to incarceration.

Prison Fellowship
Box 40562
Washington, D.C. 20016

Group founded by Watergate offender, Charles Colson.

Prisoner's Union
1315 18th Street
San Francisco, CA 94107

Composed of convicts and ex-convicts who have organized to seek prison change.

Women's Prison Association
110 Second Ave.
New York, NY 10003

Founded in 1844 to help women who have been in conflict with the law.

HELPFUL MAGAZINE ARTICLES

Because many school libraries have a rather limited selection of recent books on prisons, I have compiled a bibliography of helpful and recent magazine articles. Most school libraries have back issues of periodicals for at least a few years. I hope the following articles will be of some help to the student who wants to investigate the issue of America's prisons in more depth.

John Allen	*The Education of John Allen*, **Pscyhology Today**, October 1977, p. 97. (a criminal's biographical account)
David C. Anderson	*Co-Corrections*, **Corrections Magazine**, September 1978, p. 33.
George M. Anderson	*Criminal Justice and Women*, **America**, April 19, 1980, p. 339.
Aric Press & Diane Camper	*Strict Views of the Law*, **Time**, March 31, 1980.
Atlas World Press Review	*Breaking New Ground*, March 1979, p. 40. (special section on prisons around the world)
Philip Brickman	*Let the Punishment Fit the Crime*, **Psychology Today**, May 1977, p. 29.
Ebony	*A Double Standard of Justice*, August 1979, p. 84.
Daniel Goleman	*Proud To Be A Bleeding Heart*, **Psychology Today**, June 1978, p. 81. (a talk with Karl Menninger)
Bruce T. Grindal	*Anthropological View of Criminals and Community Rehabilitation*, **The Humanist**, July/August 1979, p. 27.
Jack Horn	*Portrait of an Arrogant Crook*, **Psychology Today**, April 1976, p. 76.
Journal of Current Social Issues	**Summer 1979 (special issue dealing with** criminals and victims)
Karl Menninger	*Doing True Justice*, **America**, July 9, 1977, p. 6.
E.H. Methvin	*A Startling New Look At The Criminal Mind*, **Readers Digest**, May 1978, p. 120.
Winston E. Moore	*Going Easy On Criminals Encourages Crime*, **Ebony**, August 1979, p. 118.

Norval Morris &
James Jacobs

Proposals For Prison Reform, 1974 (not a maga-
zine article but a helpful pamphlet published by
The Public Affairs Committee, 381 Park Avenue
So., New York, NY 10016)

The Other Side

February 1979 (special issue on prison reform)

William H. Rentschler

Let's Dismantle The Federal Prison Empire,
Corrections Magazine, March 1979, p. 72.

H. L. Richardson

Six-Time Rapist Robber Goes Free, **Conserva-
tive Digest**, April 1978, p. 45.

David Rothenberg

In Disgrace With Fortune, **America**, February 19,
1977, p. 141.

Stanton E. Samenow

*The Criminal Personality: New Concepts and
New Procedures for Change*, **The Humanist**,
September/October 1978, p. 16.

Dan Siegel

The Movement for Prisoners' Rights, **The
Progressive**, December 1979, p. 22.

Society

July/August 1974 (special issue dealing with
crime and punishment)

Time

Jail Journal, March 10, 1980, p. 62.

Time

U.S. Prisons: Myths vs. Mayhem, May 5, 1980,
p. 64. (time essay)

S. Brian Willson

More and More Prisons, **The Progressive**,
December 1979, p. 14.

James Q. Wilson

Who Is In Prison? **Commentary**, November 1976,
p. 55.

Index

Answers to Prison Poll

*Answers: 1-d, 2-c, 3-c, 4-b, 5-b, 6-a, 7-c, 8-a, 9-c, 10-c.
(Factual data from* In These Times, *National Council on Crime and Delinquency, and National Moratorium on Prison Construction.)*

ACKNOWLEDGMENTS

Illustration and Picture Credits

Pages 19, 31, 48, 103, *Prisoners' Digest International*; **Page 36**, Mike Misenheimer; **Page 46**, photographer Arnold Beckerman, reprinted with permission from Daniel & Charles Inc. Advertising; **Page 69**, artist Steve Henning; **Page 116**, United Press International Photo, **Pages 128, 130, 131**, Swedish National Prison and Probation Administration.

MEET
THE
EDITOR

David L. Bender is a history graduate from the University of Minnesota. He also has an M.A. in government from St. Mary's University in San Antonio, Texas. He has taught social problems at the high school level for several years. He is the general editor of the Opposing Viewpoints Series and has authored most of the titles in the series.